REFERENCE AND INSTRUCTIONAL SERVICES FOR INFORMATION LITERACY SKILLS IN SCHOOL LIBRARIES

REFERENCE AND INSTRUCTIONAL SERVICES FOR INFORMATION LITERACY SKILLS IN SCHOOL LIBRARIES

Third Edition

Scott Lanning

LIBRARIES UNLIMITED

AN IMPRINT OF ABC-CLIO, LLC
Santa Barbara, California • Denver, Colorado • Oxford, England

Library of Congress Cataloging-in-Publication Data

Lanning, Scott.
  [Essential reference services for today's school media specialists]
  Reference and instructional services for information literacy skills in school libraries / Scott Lanning. — Third edition.
      pages cm
  Includes bibliographical references and index.
    ISBN 978–1–61069–671–5 (pbk : alk. paper) — ISBN 978–1–61069–672–2 (ebook)
  1. School libraries—Reference services. 2. Information literacy—Study and teaching. 3. School libraries—Reference services—United States. 4. Information literacy—Study and teaching—United States. I. Title.
  Z675.S3L265 2014
  025.5'2778—dc23   2014004108

ISBN: 978–1–61069–671–5
EISBN: 978–1–61069–672–2

18 17 16 15 14   1 2 3 4 5

This book is also available on the World Wide Web as an eBook.
Visit www.abc-clio.com for details.

Libraries Unlimited
An Imprint of ABC-CLIO, LLC

ABC-CLIO, LLC
130 Cremona Drive, P.O. Box 1911
Santa Barbara, California 93116-1911

This book is printed on acid-free paper ∞

Manufactured in the United States of America

This book is dedicated to my students who keep this topic new and always have something to teach me, and to my wife, Maria. Without her support, this book would not have happened.

Contents

List of Figures

Preface

Reference librarianship has changed dramatically in the last 20 years. The whole process of finding information has undergone a fundamental shift. Print resources have given way to electronic resources hosted on the Web. Materials can be found quickly and easily. Yet finding quality information from reliable sources in the oceans of information available to us takes time, skill, and specialized knowledge. Progress has not simplified the job of reference librarians. They need to be aware of many more sources and ways of finding information than ever before.

The role of the reference librarian has changed as well. Reference librarianship is teaching. Reference librarians are on the front lines of information literacy. Each reference encounter is an opportunity to teach and tutor students in the skills and knowledge they need to find quality information. Library instruction sessions allow reference librarians to teach a class of students the skills and knowledge that we call information literacy. We know how important information literacy is to our students' success in school and how important it will be to them throughout their lives.

The reference librarian's knowledge of resources and provision of services has changed the role the library plays in the school. The school library is not just a study hall with books and a stern librarian making sure no one is talking. It is a place where students can explore and acquire information. It is a place where a teacher can learn about new technologies and how they can be used in the classroom. The reference librarian uses his or her knowledge of information literacy and library resources to help the school reach its educational goals. The reference librarian is an active participant in teaching, a colleague who shares his or her special expertise with other teachers to improve instruction throughout the school, a promoter of information resources and services, and an advocate of the importance of information literacy to students and teachers alike.

This book is aimed at those people who are interested in becoming school librarians those who want to expand their understanding of reference and instruction services and improve their reference and teaching skills. It shows these essential skills in the context of today's information literacy standards and the new, unique role that librarians play in their schools. The material in this book is designed to give you a solid foundation in all aspects of providing reference and instruction services to your students and teachers. It also helps you see the important role you play in your school and the need to promote what you do and your value in the education process.

The book focuses on information, reference skills and resources, instruction and instructional services, and assessment and value. The concepts of leadership, collaboration, and marketing are integrated in the chapters. Each chapter ends with a list of vocabulary, some questions for thoughts and discussion, and an assignment question to review and reinforce the material.

Writing this book was a wonderful learning experience, just like reference work and teaching. I hope you will enjoy this book and learn something new and valuable that will make you a better librarian. I also hope you understand that being a librarian is not only challenging but also rewarding and fun. You get to learn new things every day and have the chance to help others find joy and rewards in learning. I hope that this book will help you see the importance of what you do.

Chapter **1**

Information

In this chapter, we will examine what constitutes information, where it comes from, how it is produced, transmitted, and received, and its life cycle.

WHAT IS INFORMATION?

We all have an understanding of what information is. We use information every day of our lives, but can you define information? Here are a few definitions of information from *A Dictionary of Media and Communication* (Chandler and Munday 2011):

Often used loosely as a synonym for data, facts, or knowledge.
New or previously unknown knowledge or facts.
Knowledge acquired by learning or research.

What do you see when you look at these definitions? Do they clearly define information? Do these definitions from Merriam-Webster (2013a) help?

The communication or reception of knowledge or intelligence.
A signal or character (as in a communication system or computer) representing data.
A quantitative measure of the content of information.

Perhaps we should approach this question from a different perspective with the following definition. A *bit*:

is the primary unit for measuring information and uncertainty. The bit is a yes/no decision, which may be represented in an information system, or computer, by the two positions of a simple on–off switch. ("Bit" 2012)

Perhaps this did not help either. The definitions of information listed here mix their terminology and confuse the issue. Is information the same as knowledge as some of the definitions imply? No, it is not. Instead, we will use this definition. Information is:

Data which has been recorded, classified, organized, related, or interpreted within a framework so that meaning emerges. (McGraw-Hill Dictionary of Scientific and Technical Terms 2013)

This definition tells us that information is made up of something else, data. It also tells us that information does not have meaning unless there is a way to interpret it. For example:

1000.

This is data. It has no meaning. What if I told you it is a binary number? Now you would know that it is the number "8."Knowing that it is binary is the framework that allows us to interpret this data, though "8" is certainly a basic meaning. If we attach a "BC" or an "AD" to the end of the number, we now know that it is a year, and we can look up what events happened in that year. If we put a dollar sign in front of the number, we have a monetary value, $1,000. If we write that number on a price tag and place it on a car, the context that the data have been placed in gives significant meaning. What comes to your mind when you think of a $1,000 car? If we take that price tag and put it on a bicycle, we get a very different image and a very different meaning.

Notice that our definition of information does not mention facts. Information does not have to be factual. Information can consist of the latest water cooler gossip. In that context, 1,000 can take on whole new meanings, such meanings as the cost of the dinner your boss held to entertain a new client, the size of the bonus that only one member of your team received, or the mistaken number of boxes of paper the new secretary ordered. None of this information may be true, but it is information. There is a lot of misinformation available, which makes the evaluation of information the most important aspect of information literacy, and it will be discussed later on in this book.

Notice also that our definition does not mention knowledge. Information is not knowledge. They are two separate things. Here is our definition of information:

Knowledge is information that has been processed, integrated, assimilated, and accepted into an individual's consciousness.

This means that knowledge is an individual thing. We construct our worldview for ourselves. The information we interact with may or may not become part of who we are. We may accept or reject information, and that information may reinforce existing opinions or alter our thinking. This is illustrated in Figure 1.1.

Figure 1.1. Transformations of Data, Information, and Knowledge

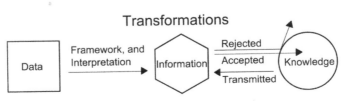

Unfortunately, knowledge cannot be passed along to others, only information, and it does not matter what method of communication we choose; the act of trying to transmit knowledge turns it into information. As the author of this book, I would like to believe that I can give you the benefit of my years of experience working in reference and instructional services. However, I cannot. I can write down what I know, but when you read it, it is information that you choose to accept or reject. If you accept some part of it, then you process the information, and it becomes part of your knowledgebase. Our parents wanted us to learn from their experience, but we still managed to make the same mistakes they did, and we repeat the same process with our children. Why does this happen?

WHERE DOES INFORMATION COME FROM?

Information can come from many sources. Information comes from your coworkers. It come from a television news broadcast or an e-mail message. It can come from a book or a magazine. No matter what source the information comes from, there is always a producer of information.

As an example, assume that a volcano erupts somewhere in the world. Is the volcano the information producer? According to our definition, the volcanic eruption is the data. The news team that shows up and reports on the devastation and loss of lives is the information producer. The volcanologists who write articles about the magnitude of the eruption are the information producers, as are the urban planners, and politicians who propose new laws regarding human settlements near volcanoes. All of these information producers have responded to the same data and produced very different information within their own unique frameworks.

The following example takes a more detailed look at an information producer. This time it is a scientist working alone in the rain forests. She has been there for many years studying the plants and gathering data. She has found new species and recorded the data on growing conditions, propagation, and chemical properties. At this point, is she an information producer?

HOW IS INFORMATION RECORDED, CLASSIFIED, AND ORGANIZED?

Our scientist records all the data she gathered in the many notebooks she kept while doing her research. Is the log of her research information or data? To our scientist, these logs may represent information, because she already possesses the knowledge to construct a framework and organize her data, but to the rest of the world, this is data.

Our scientist returns home and begins the task of organizing all these data so others can understand what she found. The first thing she does is discuss some of her findings with her colleagues. Is this information? Yes, it is, but the audience is small. Now she begins work on a paper. The paper represents her best thinking, clear and organized, on the data she has gathered and interpreted. This is clearly information, but there is another step. She must get this paper published.

The audience for this paper is other botanists like herself. It is written in the language that botanists will understand, but nonbotanists may not. To find a journal in which to publish her article, our scientist looks at *Ulrich's International Periodicals Directory* (2006) and finds 55 pages of botany journals. By selecting a journal in her field, our scientist is further classifying her information. Our scientist selects a journal and submits her paper in the hopes that it will get published.

WHERE DOES INFORMATION GET INTERPRETED AND ANALYZED?

Our scientist has already interpreted and analyzed her data to write her paper and support the conclusions she has drawn from the data. Now that she has submitted the paper to a scholarly journal, a panel of experts will review her work and check her facts. They will interpret and analyze the information that our scientist has presented to them and decide whether her work is good enough to be published in their journal. This is the peer review process that typifies scholarly publishing.

The peer reviewers find our scientist's article to be exceptional, and it gets published in their journal. Now her research is available to anyone. Persons who read her article will interpret and analyze her information for themselves, but how do they find out about her article?

HOW DOES INFORMATION GET TO YOU?

Perhaps you are a botanist, and you subscribe to the journal that published our scientist's article. If that is the case, then when the new issue arrives, you will have a copy of our scientist's article. However, if you do not subscribe to this journal, how would you find this article?

The publishing process is the important step in getting information to you. Once the information is published, you gain access to it. "Published" does not mean printed anymore. There are many ways that information can be published. It can be broadcast on the radio, the television, or the Internet. It can be published on a Web page, blog, Facebook, or Twitter account. It can be published when the information in the form of a work of art is performed on stage or exhibited at a gallery.

But what if we miss the broadcast, or we do not subscribe to that journal, or our friends and colleagues do not mention this information. Published information gets recorded and classified once again by indexing services that provide many ways to find the original information. This is the typical flow of information from producer to consumer, as illustrated in Figure 1.2.

Indexing allows us to find the information that we do not directly encounter. It provides access to the world of information that we would otherwise miss. According to Eric Schmidt, former CEO of Google, we create as much information every two days as was created from the beginning of human history to 2003 (Siegler 2013). That is a tremendous amount of information. When we have a question that needs to be answered, we need some mechanism to sort

Figure 1.2. Flow of Information from Creator to Consumer

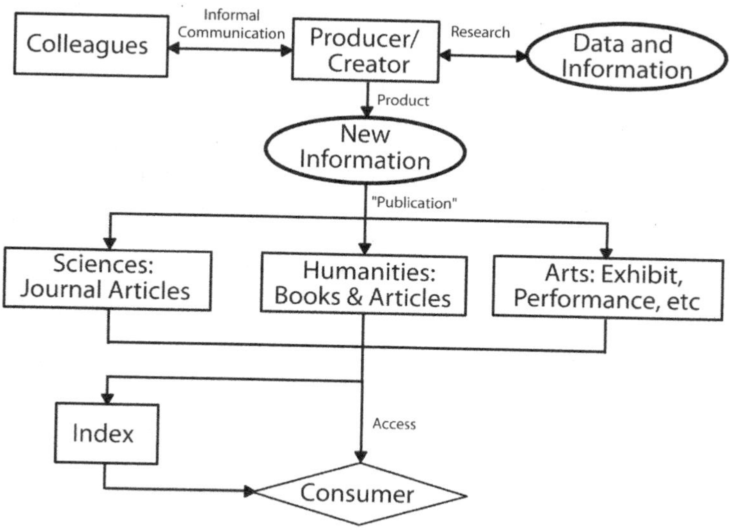

through the vast record of information. Indexes provide the means to sift that information for the answers we need.

FOUR TYPES OF INFORMATION BY AGE

We can examine the types of information available by how quickly it is published, and we can learn how this publishing schedule affects the information. The four types of information by age are news sources, journals, books, and reference sources. Figure 1.3 shows the relative times to publication for each of the information types.

News Sources—Instant Information

News sources have the shortest time to publication. Information can be presented live as it is happening on the Web, television, and radio. It can be presented the next day in a daily newspaper or on a nightly news broadcast.

Information in news sources generally has the least depth of any of the types of publications. It is often short and cursory in nature. A number of news

Figure 1.3. Time to Publication

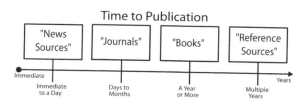

sources have a very broad scope. Daily newspapers try to cover the local, national, and world news in a few pages, whereas national news broadcasts have less than half an hour to do the same thing. Other news sources can have a narrower scope and focus on one topic or industry.

If the news source is a live broadcast of an event, another news source will often condense the information within minutes or hours of the event and give you yet another place to find the information. For example, anytime that Apple announces new products, the live event is broadcast on the Internet. Technology publications live blog the event, pulling out the informational highlights, and then post a more polished summary after the event.

News sources are important to everyone and every academic discipline. They help disseminate information to a wide audience, including a wide audience outside the information's normal discipline, and they do so quickly. News sources provide us with instant information. News, however, is often ephemeral information. It is important at that moment, but when that moment passes, so does its importance.

Journals—Current Information

Journals include such popular magazines as *Time* and *Rolling Stone*, such trade publications as *Beverage World* for the soda industry, *American Libraries* for librarians, and finally such scholarly journals as *Journal of Cell Biology* and *Journal of Information Literacy*.

Journals take longer to produce than news sources. A popular magazine may have coverage of a story only a day or two after it happened, or it may take many months to move an article through the publication process of a scholarly journal. Journals may have short "news" pieces that are the same as news sources, but journals are generally characterized by longer, in-depth articles. They have more space and/or more time to devote to their articles. Think of the differences between television news coverage of an event and a television news "magazine" coverage of that same event. Local news may give a murder two minutes of coverage, whereas a show like *48 Hours* will dedicate a full hour to the story

Journals can have a very broad scope like some news sources. More likely, they are focused on a particular topic. It may be a broad topic like fashion, or it may be a very narrow topic like cell death. Whatever the topic, there is certainly at least one journal for it.

Although journals appeal to almost everyone and all academic disciplines, they are the gold standard of scientific publishing. Information moves fast in the sciences, and it needs a responsive medium for publication. Scientific research also needs the space that journals offer to detail their research process, outcomes, and interpretations. Journals are a great source of current information.

Books—Mature Information

Books take longer to produce than news sources or journals. This is usually a consequence of their length. Books can have a broad or narrow scope and have shallow or great depth, but they are longer than their journal and news source counterparts. This gives books time to explore their topics. Books can provide a look at the current state of thinking in any discipline in a synthesized, cohesive whole, remembering the time it takes to get a book published. Books are important to the humanities. Many of the ideas and topics to be explored in the humanities are too long for a journal article, and unlike the sciences, the best thinking on a topic is not as time sensitive. The best thinking on a humanities topic may have been published 10 years ago, whereas the best thinking on a topic in the sciences may be based on a discovery that was published for the first time, yesterday. In this regard, books deal with mature information.

Reference Sources—Established Information

Reference sources are big works that generally involve a lot of people and take the longest amount of time to compile, edit, and publish. Their scope is very broad. Reference sources can try to cover all information in a broad discipline, like *McGraw-Hill Encyclopedia of Science and Technology*. Their scope can be very narrowly focused to defining all the words in a discipline like *The Penguin Dictionary of Mathematics*. These sources are good examples of the differing depths that reference sources may have. The encyclopedia will devote pages to a topic, whereas the dictionary may have only a couple of lines.

As encyclopedias have moved to an electronic publishing model, they have gained certain benefits. The basic information still took years to compile and produce, but it can now be updated very quickly as new information becomes available, instead of having to go through the print revision process that could take years for the new information to show up in a printed edition.

Reference sources deal with facts and well-established information. They are not speculative. The information provided needs to be verifiable and accurate. A reference source that does not provide accurate information will not last long in the marketplace. Reference sources are a great place to start a research project, because they provide a good overview of a topic without the length a book would have.

The information presented in a news source may lead to a journal article that changes our thinking. This in turn may lead to a book that incorporates these new ideas into established thinking. Then, years later, a reference source will include this now well-established idea into its articles.

The information will disappear from news sources about as quickly as it appeared. It will lose prominence in the journal literature next, gradually disappear from books, and finally be revised out of reference sources. In some disciplines like the sciences and medicine, this process moves quickly as new discoveries are made at an astonishing pace. In other such disciplines as the humanities and the arts, this process is considerably slower as the rate of information change is slower. It will still exist in historical archives and indexes, but for most intents and purposes, it has run its course.

Vocabulary

accepted information

books

consumer

current information

data

ephemeral information

established information	news sources
information	producer
instant information	reference sources
journals	rejected information
knowledge	time to publication
mature information	

Questions

What is information to you, and how would you define it?

Why is it not possible to transmit knowledge?

How does information get replaced?

Assignment

Give an example of information you produced, and how you transmitted it to others. Diagram the process.

Think of an example of information that you rejected. Explain why you rejected this information.

Chapter 2

Information Literacy

In this chapter, we examine information literacy and what that means. We discuss standards and models of information literacy and finally look at information literacy's connection to critical thinking.

WHAT IS INFORMATION LITERACY?

Information literacy is the ability to recognize when information is needed and then locate, evaluate, manage, and use information efficiently, effectively, and ethically to answer the need while becoming information independent and a lifelong learner.

That is our working definition, and parts of it come from the definition stated in *Presidential Committee on Information Literacy: Final Report* (2013) that is available at the American Library Association Web site and from the numerous definitions listed by Webber and Johnston (2006). These definitions are remarkably similar to each other, with only a few minor differences: Some may mention "ethics" while others do not; some may not mention "efficient" while others do. This basic agreement on what constitutes information literacy means that we can move on to the important work of teaching information literacy.

Our definition starts with recognizing an information need. This means we know we have a question, and we need to find an answer to it. The next step is locating the information that might answer our question. This is the information search. It is a process unto itself, and if this process is too difficult, complicated, or confusing, we may abandon our question. Becoming information literate should make this process easier and increase our efficiency and effectiveness in locating information.

The evaluation of information is a key step in this process. It is where we either accept or reject the information we found based on a set of criteria that we use to evaluate the quality of the information. Information literacy teaches us objective criteria to use when evaluating information that should enable us to make better decision and moderate the impact of our worldview on the information that we choose to accept or reject.

We need to manage the information we find. That means we need to store and organize our information and ideas in order that it can be retrieved easily later when we need it. We may need the information for only a brief period of time or for months or years at a time. Organization can be as simple as a stack of notes or as robust as citation manager software. Retrieving the information that we find from our files, paper, or digital means that we do not have to start our information search from the beginning.

Next, we use that information to make a decision, to answer our question. In the case of a student with a research question, he or she would then use that information to write a research paper or create his or her project. Information needs to be used ethically. If an idea originated with another person and you restate it, you need to give credit for the idea to its originator, its information producer. For students, this means citing the information sources they used in creating their papers or projects. The whole process needs to be effective and efficient. We need to find the right information and find it with a minimum of wasted time.

Finally, information literacy is the pursuit of becoming information independent and a lifelong learner. As educators, we value learning. We want our students to understand that they should never stop learning and that asking, then answering questions for themselves keeps them engaged with life and expands their horizons and their understanding of the world. All democracies need informed and engaged citizens, and our businesses need productive, efficient employees who know how to learn and update their skills. What would happen if you chose to stop learning? How long would it take for what you know to become obsolete and turn into an information need?

To enable all of these benefits of information literacy, we must learn how to become information independent. This does not mean free from information. Information independence is freedom from a dependence on only one or a few information sources. It is the knowledge that many information sources exist and that they have value. It is the ability to find information for ourselves from multiple information sources beyond the usual ones that we are exposed to, then evaluate, and interpret this information for ourselves. It is the essential ingredient in becoming a critical thinker.

WHAT DOES IT MEAN TO BE LITERATE?

If you believe the literature, there are many different kinds of literacies that we need to know to get through our daily lives. Here is a partial list:

visual literacy

digital literacy

financial literacy

geographic literacy

media literacy

scientific literacy

health literacy

computer literacy

spatial literacy

historical literacy

STEM literacy

transliteracy

meta literacy

information literacy.

Are these all legitimate literacies? Or do these beg the question, what does it mean to be literate? Ivan Sutherland is a computing pioneer who created Sketchpad. He was asked if he thought it was necessary to teach children to be digitally literate by teaching them to program. "Not necessary," he answered. "Do kids need to learn to drive? Probably. But do they need to know how to repair an engine? No" ("A Computing Pioneer Looks to the Next Frontier" 2013).

What does it mean to be literate? The first definition of literate in the *Oxford English Dictionary* is:

Of a person, society, etc.: acquainted with letters or literature; erudite, learned, lettered. (2013)

Merriam-Webster is more direct with its first definition: "educated, cultured." It is definition 1b that mentions the ability to read and write (Merriam-Webster, Inc. 2013a). Transliteracy, one of the literacies mentioned in the list provided earlier, is a new concept that is "concerned with what it means to be literate in the 21st century" with a focus on using all forms of media (Ipri 2010). Our definitions of literate do not mention any medium, and they do not mention what it means to be educated, or "learned. Those are meanings that have changed over time.

STEM literacy is a very popular topic in education right now. STEM stands for science, technology, engineering, and mathematics. It is defined as using the principles of scientific thought to solve complex problems, think critically, and seek data (Wladawsky-Berger 2012). Perhaps it is good enough to say that the education system should produce literate students and that a literate person is one who can participate effectively in society. The concept of literate is big enough to stand in for all of the individual literacies. In that case, what should we call information literacy?

THEORIES OF INFORMATION LITERACY AND BEHAVIOR

Theories of information behavior try to explain why we do what we do when it comes to the search for information and how those search systems work. Information behavior theories examine our motivation to seek information in the first place, and what impact who we are and what we are hoping to find has on our behavior. They also examine the impact of information systems on the search and results. These theories can be useful in helping us understand the big picture of the information-seeking process and where information literacy fits in that process.

Practice Theory

"A practice is an organised [sic] nexus of human activities and it is through practice that understanding and intelligibility occur. All practices occur within a social field and in doing so reflect the knowledge claims that are embodied within that field" (Lloyd 2010). Practice theory is located within a social context that impacts information-seeking behavior, the interpretation of information, and sharing of information. Competency with information literacy skills is also defined by the social context in which it exists. What is competent information literacy practice at work or for a science class may not be competent for an information literacy class.

Information Behavior Wheel

Natalya Godbold (2013) based her theory of information behavior on a combination of theories from Thomas Wilson's Information Behavior and Brenda Dervin's Theory of Sensemaking. In this theory, an information need illuminates a gap in knowledge. That gap can be crossed, closed, or ignored depending on the seeker's worldview and an understanding of what closing the gap means to that worldview. Godbold's model is nonlinear. As she says, "The order of information seeking tasks may be reversed or convoluted, and includes dead-ends, changes of direction, iteration, abandonment, and beginning again" (2013).

Activity Theory

Activity theory (AT), or cultural–historical activity theory, uses the ideas of motivation, goal, activity, tools, object, outcome, rules, community, and division of labor to examine behavior. AT examines how we operate within a specific context (the cultural, historical, and social aspects of a given system or discipline), either cooperatively or alone using the tools, and rules of that context to find our answers. Context has significant impact on the tools available and the rules or social norms that guide the behavior. Wilson (2006) examines the major threads of AT and combines them into a model that can be used to examine information behavior. AT as expressed by Wilson includes feedback loops throughout the process that provide the ability to change course.

STANDARDS FOR INFORMATION LITERACY

Standards are requirements. They are goals that need to be met. Information literacy standards represent a level of achievement that needs to be met. Each individual standard consists of multiple parts: the standard that needs to be met and a list of skills necessary to meet the standards, outcomes from achieving the standards, or a means to assess compliance with the standard. Aside from the standard itself, these other parts are optional and vary from standard to standard. There are a number of standards for information literacy. A few of them are listed here.

Twenty-First-Century Fluencies

These standards take a broad view of education and examine what we need to know about how to be productive members of the new digital society. The five fluencies are solution, creative, collaboration, media, and information. The fluencies are placed within the context of global digital citizenship. Information fluency is of particular interest to us. It forms a model and is included in Figure 2.1. The definition of information fluency is "the ability to unconsciously and intuitively interpret information in all forms and formats in order to extract the essential knowledge, perceive its meaning and significance, and use it to complete real-world tasks" (Crockett, Jukes, and Churches 2011).

The Common Core State Standards

The Common Core State Standards (CCSS) were written by the National Governors Association Center for Best Practices and the Council of Chief State School Officers with the idea of improving education across the country with clear expectation and challenging goals ("The Standards" 2012). Forty-five states have adopted the standards since their publication in 2010 ("In the States" 2012). The standards have been benchmarked, and they are designed to improve college and work readiness (Morris 2012).

The standards have two main parts: Mathematics Standards and English Language Arts Standards that consists of reading and writing across the curriculum. It is this last standard area that is so important for librarians. It includes an emphasis on critical reading of texts, both literary and informational, and research and writing skills across disciplines (Morris 2012). With its focus on critical thinking, use of texts, multidisciplinary research, and its wide adoption, the CCSS is of vital importance to school librarians.

Standards for the 21st-Century Learner

The American Association of School Librarians (AASL) developed the *Standards for the 21st-Century Learner* in 2007 (American Association of School Librarians 2007). There are four main standards:

Inquire, think critically, and gain knowledge.
Draw conclusions, make informed decisions, apply knowledge to new situations, and create new knowledge.
Share knowledge and participate ethically and productively as members of our democratic society.
Pursue personal and aesthetic growth. (Langhorne, Rehmke, and Iowa City Community School District 2011)

Each standard is further subdivided into four categories: Skills, which are the abilities needed to meet the standards; Dispositions in Action, which are the learners' attitudes; Responsibilities, which are good and ethical information behaviors; and Self-Assessment Strategies, which evaluate outcomes at each standard.

The AASL standards are also very important. They were developed by our professional organization that knows what we do and how important it is. AASL standards have been appropriate and useful standards for school librarians for years. Does this mean that we have to choose between competing standards? No. You can have multiple standards in place at any one time. To make it easy to implement both the 21st-Century standards and the CCSS standards, the AASL has developed a crosswalk between the standards (American Association of School Librarians 2013). These guides map 21st-Century standards to CCSS and vice versa. That enables you to look at the 21st-Century standards that you meet with a particular library instruction session and see which CCSS standards are also being met.

MODELS OF INFORMATION LITERACY

Models are used as a means to reach the goals set by standards. They are a way to teach a process that may include learning a set of skills. A model is not a theory. Whereas a theory examines the big picture, models show how to accomplish a specific task. There are many models of information literacy. Only a few are listed here.

Information Search Process

Developed by Carol Kuhlthau, the information search process includes seven steps that move the researcher through initiation, selection of a topic to presentation, assessment of the process, and outcome. As the researcher progresses through the process, he or she should gain confidence with his or her research and topic (MacDonald and Darrow 2013).

Stripling and Pitts Research Process Model

Stripling and Pitts' research process model has 10 steps from start to finish. Each step includes reflective questions that help students evaluate their work ("REACTS Stripling and Pitts Research Process Model" 2011). This is a feedback loop.

Seven Pillars

The Seven Pillars model was developed by the Society of College, National and University Libraries (SCONUL) in the United Kingdom. The SCONUL model is often presented in a circular diagram to show that it is a nonlinear process (SCONUL Working Group on Information Literacy 2011).

Pathways to Knowledge

Pathways to Knowledge was developed by Marjorie L. Pappas and Ann E. Tepe under the sponsorship of Follett. It was designed with K-12 in mind. Students are encouraged to evaluate and reassess at each step along the way ("Pathways to Knowledge" 2013). This is one of the few models that mention information management.

The Big6 Skills

The Big6 was developed by Mike Eisenberg and Bob Berkowitz, and like Pathways, it is aimed at K-12 students. According to its Web site, Big6 is the most popular information literacy model in the world ("Big6 Skills Overview" 2013). It is a linear model that takes you through the research process.

Figure 2.1 shows the basic steps of each of the information literacy models mentioned here.

CRITICAL THINKING AND INFORMATION LITERACY

Critical thinking is an educational philosophy that originated with Socrates (McCrink and Melton 2009). It involves asking and answering questions to arrive at reasoned conclusions. Robert Ennis introduced the idea of critical thinking to the modern education debate with his new model and push for the teaching of it in 1962 ("Critical Thinking" 1996). Critical thinking has much in common with information literacy.

One definition of critical thinking is "reasonable reflective thinking focused on deciding what to believe or do," and it includes such factors as being open-minded, judging credibility of sources, judging quality of arguments and evidence, formulating hypotheses, and drawing conclusions when warranted (Ennis 2012). Critical thinking involves the higher-order thinking of analysis, synthesis, and evaluation (McCrink and Melton 2009). It is central to the aims of education ("Critical Thinking" 1996), and it is "imperative for the human experience and the pursuit of a democratic world order" (McCrink and Melton 2009).

The claims for critical thinking certainly sound similar to the claims for information literacy, and critical thinking is included in the definition of STEM literacy. What does this tell us about the relationship between critical thinking and information literacy? Critical thinking is important to all disciplines. It is a way of thinking about an issue. It is a part of information literacy, just as it is a part of STEM literacy, but it is only a part. Information literacy encompasses more ideas and behaviors, while also being more specific about the information-seeking process. Thus, both are important across all academic disciplines and in our lives. Weiner found in his study of both concepts that information literacy touched on all of the levels of thinking in Bloom's taxonomy and that critical thinking tends to be more internalized, and discipline specific, while information literacy has a public, more cross-disciplinary aspect (Weiner 2011). Information literacy is also important to all disciplines. So when we teach information literacy, we are also teaching critical thinking.

Figure 2.1. Models of Information Literacy

Information Fluency	Information Search Process	Research Process	Seven Pillars	Pathways to Knowledge	Big6
1. Ask 2. Access 3. Analyze 4. Apply 5. Assess	1. Initiation 2. Selection 3. Exploration 4. Formulation 5. Collection 6. Presentation 7. Assessment	1. Choose a broad topic 2. Get an overview 3. Narrow the topic 4. Develop thesis statement 5. Formulate questions 6. Plan for research 7. Find, analyze, evaluate 8. Evaluate evidence 9. Establish conclusions 10. Create and present final product	1. Identify 2. Scope 3. Plan 4. Gather 5. Evaluate 6. Manage 7. Present	1. Appreciation and Enjoyment 2. Presearch 3. Search 4. Interpretation 5. Communication 6. Evaluation	1. Task Definition 2. Information-Seeking Strategies 3. Location and Access 4. Use of Information 5. Synthesis 6. Evaluation

Vocabulary

critical thinking	lifelong learner
effective use of information	literacy
efficient use of information	management of information
ethical use of information	models of information literacy
information independence	standards for information literacy
information literacy	STEM literacy
information need	theories of information literacy
information search	use of information

Questions

What constitutes unethical use of information both within and outside of class?

What did it mean to be educated 500 years ago versus 100 years ago versus today?

What is the difference between an information theory and an information model?

Assignment

Pick an information theory, standard, and model that you think are best and defend your position.

Analyze the Models of Information Literacy in Figure 2.1 and describe the similarities and differences between the models.

Chapter **3**

How Students Find Information

In this chapter, we will look at student information-seeking behaviors and how these behaviors differ from the models mentioned in Chapter 2.

BECOMING INFORMATION LITERATE

Students believe that they are good information seekers (Cox and Androit 2009; Georgas 2013). They rate their search abilities highly. In a report on college students' self-rating of their search skills, students rated their skill more highly before taking a research course than after (Cox and Androit 2009). Another study supports these findings that students overrate their information-seeking abilities and showed that the large majority of students scored in the "below proficient" range on a standardized information literacy skills test, only a few scored in the "proficient" range, and none scored in the "advanced" range (Coates 2013). What does this say about the information literacy instruction that students are receiving in K-12 education?

College students for course assignments turn to assigned materials, Google, and then library databases for their research. Next, it is instructors, classmates, encyclopedias, and friends, and then librarians (Head and Eisenberg 2009b). In the same study, Head and Eisenberg mention that students rely on "the same few information resources" regardless of subject and whether the need is for an assignment or personal reasons. In other words, learned information behaviors result in habits that hurt students' ability to find relevant information, and these habits are hard to break. In a study of 200 education majors, Martin (2008) found that students use their preferred sources and that information literacy instruction did not affect students' choices of resources. Minkel (2002) quotes a study by the Pew Research Center that found "94 percent of students between the ages of 12 and 17 with access to the web use it for

19

research, with 71 percent citing it as their main source of information for school projects." This study is old, but has anything changed since it was written?

In another study, Head and Eisenberg (2009a) state that "research seems to be far more difficult to conduct in the digital age than it did in previous times." How can this be? In the pre-database era, searching involved pouring through multiple volumes of print indexes to find citations to journal articles. Then the journals needed to be found and the articles located within them. This process took hours. Today with full-text databases and Google, this process takes only minutes. Unfortunately, this new and efficient process returns more information than could ever be found by using print indexes.

Information seeking begins with motivation. For students, that motivation is often external. They receive an assignment. Motivation can also be internal, which is a desire to know. Heinström identified three levels of inquiry based on student motivation in middle and high schools. These levels are surface, strategic, and deep (Heinström 2006). Surface searching is quick and designed to meet the conditions of the assignment. It is extrinsically motivated. Strategic is deeper searching, designed not only to meet the conditions of the assignment but also to garner good grades. It is both intrinsically and extrinsically motivated. Finally, deep searching is searching that goes beyond the assignment to fill an information desire within the student and is intrinsically motivated. Heinström noted that students would change their level of searching depending on the topic and whether it interested them. However, Head and Eisenberg (2010b) noted that students working on course assignments cared most about passing the course, completing the assignments, and getting a good grade, in that order. The external motivation of course work is a powerful influence on information seeking.

A number of issues collide here to produce poor information-seeking behavior. Our search habits are formed by easy-to-use search tools that return millions of hits on any topic in seconds, an informal network for getting help that puts expert experience at the bottom of the list, and generally weak, external motivations to seek. This is how we become information literate!

INFORMATION OVERLOAD BARRIER

Two major barriers to information literacy are addressed here. The first is information overload or the retrieval of too much information. A study of college students mentions that their biggest challenges with their information search for course assignments are information overload and too much irrelevant information (Georgas 2013). Relevance is an important concept in information retrieval. In general, the more information you find, the lower the percentage of relevant information. One behavior to avoid this problem as outlined by Olof and Francke was for students to search Google, scan the first page of results, and follow the first link which was often to Wikipedia (2009).

Students do evaluate Web sites, and they use legitimate criteria. This is good news for school librarians' information literacy instruction program. The top three criteria according to Head and Eisenberg (2010b) are currency, authority, and domain (.edu, .com, .gov). The research did not say how these standards were applied, and some would argue that authority is more important than currency in many cases. Students also learn to assess credibility within the context of the assignment and what their teacher wants to see, and they also judge the credibility of a Web site by its "various architectural traits," the look, feel, organization, and navigability of the site (Sundin and Francke 2009). Unfortunately, this means that students work to the assignment, just as teachers teach to the test, and a professional-looking Web site will garner some credibility whether it deserves it or not. It is easy to see why evaluation of information and its source is one of the key issues in information literacy.

SYSTEMIC BARRIERS

Library resources offer their unique challenges to good searching. This is a context or system as mentioned in theories of information-seeking behavior that students need to learn how to operate within. This can be difficult. Library resources have their unique sets of rules. They are more specialized in terms of topical focus and types of information covered and offer many more options to search. In other words, students need to know that the library catalog finds only such materials as books, media, and journal titles that the library owns. To find articles within journals, students must turn to a journal database. They must know the rules and practices of searching the database, and they need to understand that the database may not return full-text information.

To make matters more difficult, libraries have multiple databases that need to be located on the library's Web site, and each database may have slight differences in how search is implemented. Libraries have tried to make navigating their system easier with a search box on their home page that is set to conduct a search of a specific resource or set of resources. This is the default search. Virginia Commonwealth University increased the size of its home page search box, and it received 100 percent more usage (Lown, Sierra, and Boyer 2013). The default search of a home page search box attracts the heaviest use, even if it is not appropriate to the task at hand. For example, if there is a tabbed search box on the home page where the default tab is the catalog and the second tab is a journal database, most searches will be performed in the catalog, even if article information is needed. If there is a search box to look for information on the library Web site, this can be confused with the search box that is set up to search a library resource, and students will use the home page search box to look for information about the library (Teague-Rector and Ghaphery 2008).

STUDENT INFORMATION-SEEKING BEHAVIOR

This is the general model of student information-seeking behavior painted by the information provided earlier.

1. Course assignment creates an information need.
2. Search starts with Google.
3. First page of results is consulted.
4. First item on the list is examined.
5. If this first item is not Wikipedia, then Wikipedia is consulted.
6. Web sites are evaluated for currency, authority, domain, and design.
7. If this is not enough, use a library database that has been used before.

8. If problems are encountered, ask classmates, friends, and the teacher for help in that order.
9. Find enough citations to satisfy assignment.
10. Search is stopped.

This is student information literacy behavior, but does it really represent information literate behavior or something else? How far is this model from the ideal? How close is it to minimally acceptable search behavior?

WHY INFORMATION LITERACY?

The theories and models of information literacy discussed earlier all mention the importance of information literacy. Information literacy is critical to academic success, work, life, and society. We need to be information literate to function successfully in a globally connected world. However, actual search behavior is far from ideal. It does not contain much critical thinking, is bound by habit, and leaves expert help out of the equation.

If we are to reach the lofty goals set by information literacy standards, then students need library services more than ever to reach these goals. Reference services and information literacy instruction are two ways to impart information literacy skills.

Vocabulary

authority

context

currency

default search

design

domain

evaluation

extrinsic motivation

home page search box

information overload

intrinsic motivation

system

systemic barriers

Questions

What does it mean to be information illiterate? How would you find answers to your questions?

Why do students overestimate their search skills?

How do library sources mediate information overload?

What other systemic barriers to information seeking are there?

Assignment

Create a student information-seeking model that meets what you believe to be the minimal requirements of good information seeking. Explain and defend each step.

Chapter 4

Reference Services and Information Literacy

In this chapter, we examine the purpose of reference services and how they fit in the school library and with information literacy.

REFERENCE'S ROLE IN THE SCHOOL LIBRARY

There have been many significant changes in libraries and library services that have been driven by technology. However, the goal of reference services has not changed: to help our customers utilize library resources and services to their fullest potential.

To reach this goal, we provide answers to questions from our collection of reliable sources. We direct our customers to library resources or services that will answer their information needs, and we instruct them in the effective, efficient, and ethical use of library resources.

The job description of the reference librarian as "professional question answerer" is unique. Although it is unlikely that your job description includes this exact phrase, it will include something about providing services to your customers. We do get paid to answer questions. That is what reference librarians do. The tools we use to provide those answers have changed and will continue to change, but in any case, we provide services to find answers or help our customers find answers to their questions.

REFERENCE'S ROLE IN INFORMATION LITERACY

One of our responsibilities as school librarians is to help our students become information literate. When a student asks a reference question, we have the perfect opportunity to teach them information literacy skills while answering their information need. It is the "teachable moment." That ideal moment when students' interest and need are high, so too is their willingness to learn.

It is at this moment that we can introduce students to library resources and show them how the context of information seeking works. This means everything from showing them library databases, how to select search terms, and execute their search. It means helping students find a topic, get the background information they need to understand it, and explore aspects of it through reference resources. It involves teaching our students the ethical use of information, how to cite their sources, and every other aspect of information literate behavior. Finally, it *is* about answering questions *and* encouraging more questions.

The reference transaction is not just an opportunity to reach students at the teachable moment but also a chance for students to receive one-on-one tutoring. This is not a unique experience for students, but it is standard operating procedure for libraries. However, it should signal to the students that the librarian is their research friend who is always available to provide assistance. Individualized instruction at the point of need is a very powerful tool for imparting information literacy skills.

There is more to a school librarian's job than answering reference questions, of course. There is collection development, cataloging, monitoring budgets, and working with teachers, among other things. All of these activities have something in common. They are all done in the service of information literacy. This may not seem like the case on first blush, but ask why you catalog books? Why do you choose to arrange your electronic resources in that way on your Web site? Why do you write guides to using your library or evaluating information? Why do you collaborate with teachers on research assignments?

You can answer these questions in a way that does not support information literacy. You write guides so you do not have to repeat yourself. You work with teachers to make your job easier and prevent surprises. These are legitimate answers, but they are not the best answers to the questions. You do all these things to help students and teachers with their information needs. You buy resources to answer questions. You catalog and organize these resources to make them discoverable. You write guides to help students to use these resources, and you work with teachers to ensure not only curricular goals are being met but that information literacy goals are being met as well, while helping students produce better assignments.

THE REFERENCE EXPERIENCE AND THE USER EXPERIENCE

User experience is the overall impact of the library and its personnel on the customer. It involves the sightlines when the customer walks in the door. What is the first thing that he or she sees, and what impression does it make on him or her? How is the customer treated by the staff? Is it easy to find resources and get help? Is there a nice place to sit and work? Does the customer walk away with the information he or she needs? Did the customer have a good experience?

Ensuring that customers have a good user experience is important to a library. A good user experience means repeat business. Repeat business means good word of mouth and an expanding customer base. It means your services are valued and you are earning a deserved, good reputation. A good reputation leads to even more business.

The reference experience is just a part of the overall user experience. It is an important part, because it involves interaction with the customer. While sightlines, seating, colors of the walls, and layout of the library impact the user experience, none of these will have as powerful an impact as a personal interaction. The reference transaction is a complex interaction. Ensuring that it goes well is difficult. There are many factors involved in the transaction, and it can fail at any one of them. Even if the reference transaction does not find the answer wanted, it can still be a good user experience for the customer.

How do we ensure that our customers have a good experience when they ask a reference question? Our behaviors and attitudes are critical. If we are having a bad day and are frustrated, we cannot let that attitude show when we are helping a customer, or they will have a negative experience. We need to be polite, courteous, and inviting. We need to set aside our problems and our personal biases. We need to act like the professionals we are.

GUIDELINES FOR PERFORMANCE

Performance guidelines help us understand how we need to behave. The Reference and User Services Association developed *Guidelines for Behavioral Performance of Reference and Information Service Providers*. There are five broad categories of behaviors:

1. Approachability.
2. Interest.
3. Listening/inquiring.
4. Searching.
5. Follow-up (Reference and User Services Association 2004).

Each of the categories is further subdivided, giving general behaviors and behaviors specific to in-person and remote transactions. The guidelines follow a general model of the reference transaction, which we will examine in detail in Chapter 6. Approachability comes first. Without approachability there is no reference transaction. Approachability means being available and visible. It means presenting a welcoming appearance. It means not looking busy or harried. It means making eye contact, smiling, and offering a greeting.

Interest is facing the customer and giving him or her your undivided attention. You also need to let the customer know that you understand his or her question. You should not continue typing nor keep looking down at your work. You need to maintain eye contact and stop what you are doing.

Listening/inquiring is the question negotiation phase of the reference transaction. This is where you clarify and determine the extent of the customer's information needs. You discover what the customer is after by asking open, closed-ended questions and restating their question. This process should lead to a clear idea of the kinds and amount of information needed, which leads to the next step.

Searching is where you put your information literacy skills and knowledge to use. You construct an effective and efficient search strategy to meet the customer's needs. Either you help the customer implement that strategy, or you run the search yourself depending on the nature of the question and the customer's abilities.

The final guideline is follow-up. Like all the behaviors, follow-up is important. Follow-up is also simple. After you help a customer start his or her information search, you check back in with him or her to see how he or she is doing. You ask the customer if he or she needs any more help or have any other questions or new questions. If he or she does not at that time, you ask him or her to stop by your desk if any questions do arise.

Follow-up is a powerful tool in creating a positive user experience. It is an action that shows you care about the customer's information need. Combine all the behaviors listed in the guidelines with a positive and professional attitude, and your customers will have a good user experience of your reference services, and you will have met your professional standards.

Vocabulary

approachability

follow-up

interest

listening/inquiring

professionalism

question negotiation

reference experience

reference transaction

searching

teachable moment

user experience

Questions

What do you think is the connection between reference services and information literacy?

Think about a time that you received bad customer service. Why was the transaction bad? What could have been done to make it a positive experience?

How does a negative user experience impact that customer's future behavior and the library?

What does it mean to be a professional?

Assignment

Pick one of the behaviors from the guidelines that you think is the most important behavior for a successful reference transaction. Explain why it is the most important and defend your position. Would you make a different choice of behavior if you were picking the most important one for creating a positive user experience? Why or why not?

Chapter **5**

Traditional and Contemporary Reference Services

In this chapter, we examine the various means to provide reference services and focus on the technology used to provide services. We also discuss how to implement services based on new technologies and how to determine if a new technology is viable.

REFERENCE SERVICES

Although the goal of reference services has not changed over the years, the tools we have to achieve that goal have changed dramatically. Traditional reference services consisted of in-person reference and telephone reference. This did not change for many years. As such a well-established norm, it is hard to imagine that it was ever different than this, but it was. At one point in time, the telephone was a new technology. It prompted a librarian to comment about implementing telephone reference service, "The difficulties are very great. Its problems are considerably different" (Conference, Meeting, and Association 1907). Now the telephone is just one of many tools in the reference tools box, and the "norm" has changed. Technology has changed reference services just as it has changed our lives. It has enabled new ways to find and share information with our customers.

E-MAIL

The first of new services that technology brought to reference was e-mail. E-mail reference services were an outgrowth of the personal computer revolution of the early 1980s. Kathy Niemeler (1983) reported that "1 percent of the home users and 19 percent of the business users" would have a communication option on their computers, which refers to a modem, and an e-mail service provider. This was bleeding-edge technology. How many libraries could afford to develop a service that reaches out to only 1 percent of its customers?

E-mail reference services were simple, in that all you need to provide the service was an e-mail address. Customers could e-mail their questions to the library, and a librarian would respond usually within a specified time. With the advent of the Web, form-based e-mail services were developed, which allowed the library to ask its customers for information to help it provide an answer. The Internet Public Library (http://www.ipl.org/div/askus/) runs an e-mail reference service, and its form is a model of information gathering before the questions is asked to help librarians provide the best possible answer.

E-mail is an example of an asynchronous communication. It does not take place in real time. This has a negative impact on the reference transaction. Librarians cannot ask clarifying questions and get immediate feedback just as they can with an in-person reference interview. If clarifying questions need to be asked, the e-mail transaction may go on for days. An advantage that e-mail offers is its written nature. It leaves a trail that can be referred to for clarification with the customer and analyzed for training and evaluation purposes.

CHAT, INSTANT MESSAGING, AND TEXT MESSAGING

Chat reference services followed e-mail as the next new tool for providing reference services. It was followed by instant messaging and then text messaging services. Chat reference came into being around 2000. On first seeing a live chat service, Karen Schneider (2000) noted that she had not "seen anything this important or significant for librarianship" since the Web browser. These services address the asynchronous problem of e-mail reference, providing synchronous, real-time communication.

Chat software can be simple, allowing only typed messages to be exchanged. It can also be sophisticated and include features like cobrowsing, where the librarian and the customer can view the same live Web site and watch as one or the other navigates about that site, or pushing pages where the librarian can send a live Web page to the patron to view and explore. The real-time nature enables the librarian to conduct a reference interview and receive feedback from the customer about the relevance of the information found. There are such software programs as LibraryH3lp (http://libraryh3lp.com/) that aggregate instant messaging services from Yahoo! and MSN and text messaging services, while providing a chat interface that can be embedded in any Web page.

Chat reference spawned such cooperative services as AskNow for California libraries, which is now defunct, and such ventures as QuestionPoint (http://www.questionpoint.org/) from OCLC. For a commitment of time and/or money on the part of the library, the library would receive a 24/7 reference service for its customers. Many chat services have the ability to create logs of transactions, an electronic paper trail, similar to e-mail reference, that may be examined for evaluation and training purposes. Unlike e-mail, the logs provide more information, because of the real-time nature of the transaction and the ability to conduct a reference interview. The logs may also show recurring popular questions. You can use this information to create resources to answer those questions.

Although all this sounds good, there are problems. The use of logs for performance evaluations may make library staff very uncomfortable. Creating a database of frequently asked questions takes time and becomes one more resource you have to remember to search when looking for answers. Steve Coffman, one of chat's biggest supporters, turned away from chat, saying that most chat services "are not cost effective" because of staff, software costs, technical issues, and low use. To make matters worse, chat questions take "twice as long to answer" (Tenopir 2004).

SOCIAL MEDIA

When people talk about Web 2.0, they are referring to cooperative, interactive Web services. The most prominent ones that come to mind immediately are Facebook (https://www.facebook.com), Twitter (https://www.twitter.com), and YouTube (http://www.youtube.com), but there are many others. Wikis, blogs, RSS feeds, Pinterest (https://pinterest.com), and Flickr (http://www.flickr.com) also fall into this category.

Social media has been used to great effect by libraries in promoting events and services and in providing library news. Creating videos and interactive tutorials that show students where to find information and how to use a resource is another use of social media. Libraries have also used their Facebook pages and Twitter accounts for answering reference questions. This is an asynchronous reference service model. Questions and answers can be made public, and that should help others with similar information needs, but be sure that you make enough changes to the transcript to protect the identity and privacy of the customer.

TRENDS AND TECHNOLOGY

There have been many new technologies and trends in library services. Following fashion can be fun, but it costs a lot of money and time. Which services and ideas will last long enough to make your investment payoff? Myspace (https://myspace.com) once dominated the social networking landscape, then all but disappeared, and now is trying to make a comeback but is at 340 on the list of most visited Web sites (Alexa 2013a). Facebook (https://www.facebook.com) is number one on that list, but has it peaked? Has it begun to lose customers, or is it continuing to grow? Will it go the way of Myspace when something new comes along, or will it last as long as the telephone?

The information in Figure 5.1 was gathered by searching Library, Information Science & Technology Abstracts (LISTA). Phrase searching and/or subject searching was used to get the results. The results are not perfect but are good enough for comparison purposes. Figure 5.2 shows the table of values that were found during the searches, which provides another way to look at the information.

Figure 5.1. Topic Hits in LISTA

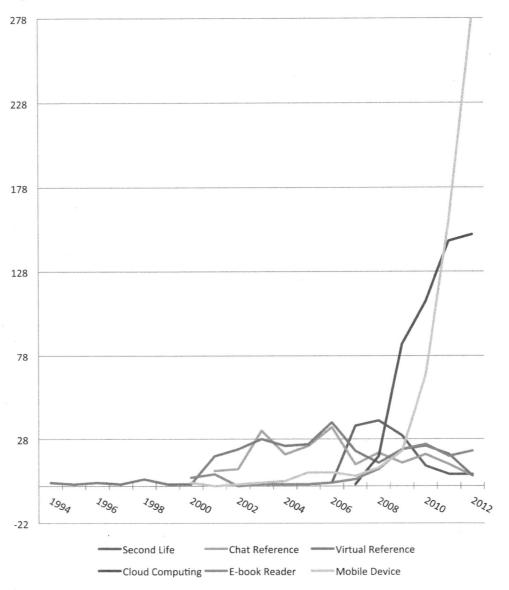

Second Life (http://www.secondlife.com) was going to be the next big thing in education and librarianship, but that did not come to pass. It is a virtual world with virtual schools and libraries among the many places that you explore with an avatar, a user-created character. By examining the graph and table, you can see that Second Life sprung on the scene, garnered a lot of talk, and then quickly started to fade. Chat reference appears to follow a similar pattern, articles peaked in 2006, and the trend in publication has been down. However, there is a difference between the two: Second Life is fading away, but

Figure 5.2. Table of Values for Figure 5.1

	Second Life	Chat Reference	Virtual Reference	Cloud Computing	E-Book Reader	Mobile Device
1994			2			
1995			1			
1996			2			
1997			1			
1998			4			
1999			1			
2000			1		5	2
2001		9	18		7	0
2002		10	22		0	1
2003		33	28		1	2
2004		19	24		1	3
2005		24	25		1	8
2006	2	35	38		2	8
2007	36	13	21	1	4	6
2008	39	20	14	18	10	11
2009	30	14	22	85	22	21
2010	12	19	24	110	25	66
2011	7	13	19	146	18	158
2012	7	6	6	150	21	278

chat is commonplace. Chat reference may be seeing less publishing because of its market penetration.

How can you tell if something is a technology fade, or if it is here to stay? Clearly, cloud computing and mobile devices are garnering much attention in the literature of our profession, with mobile devices really taking off in the last couple of years. This is an indication that these are important topics in our field, at least for now. To determine if these are trends or important technologies for you to consider, you need to ask questions.

IMPLEMENTING NEW REFERENCE SERVICES

Implementing new services based on new technology is a process that should be carefully planned to give the service the best chance to succeed. Start the planning process by evaluating which services best fit with your library and reference mission. Think about what your customers use and what they want. Which service do you think you can best implement. What are your colleagues in other schools offering, and can you count on them to be your expert help if you choose to implement the same service? Is there a consortium you can join or one you can start to facilitate financial and technical support?

Consider the staffing and workload implications of the various options you are considering. How much staff time needs to be devoted to the service to make it a success, planning for both the amount of time it will take to implement the service and the amount of time it takes to run, update, maintain, or monitor the service. Do you have the staff resources to fully engage with the service? Where will the service be performed, at the desk while trying to help others or in the back? When will the service be offered? What training do you and your staff need? How will you evaluate your staff's or your performance in using this service? Most school librarians do not have a lot of time to spare, or a lot of staff to take on the responsibilities of the new service. So, you need to consider these questions closely.

What are the technical requirements of the service? Hardware requirements are not much of an issue anymore. School libraries have Internet access, and modern computers should provide plenty of processing power to run Web 2.0 services. You should consider other technical aspects, like what expertise does it take to run the service and whom to call if there are technical problems that keep the service from working correctly or from working at all. Does the service need to be hosted on your equipment, or does the provider host the service, and what does that mean to your library?

With all of these questions answered, you can think about how you are going to implement your service. You can develop your policies and procedures that will guide your service to meet your reference goals within the context of the service being offered. You need to consult your license agreements to see what information you can offer to whom from which of your sources. You need to have a marketing plan for this new service to establish awareness and develop a customer base. Finally, you must plan to evaluate the service after a set trial period and answer more questions. Is the service meeting your needs and your customers' needs? Is it being used and is it cost effective? If all the answers are positive, then you have a successful new service.

The International Federation of Library Associations and Institutions (IFLA) has created the *IFLA Digital Reference Guidelines* that cover everything you need to consider when planning for a digital service (IFLA 2013). Search the literature to find one of the many articles that describe how services were implemented in other libraries, and talk to your colleagues. These are a valuable source of information that can point out issues you may not have considered. Finally, do not forget the Reference and User Services Association Guidelines (mentioned in Chapter 4) that discuss appropriate, professional behavior for reference transactions regardless of the medium.

MAKING WISE TECHNOLOGY DECISIONS

A final question to ask yourself about technology adoption is whether this technology is bleeding edge, leading edge, or trailing edge, and what that means to you and your library. Figure 5.3 illustrates Everett Rogers's idea of Diffusion

Figure 5.3. Diffusion of Innovations

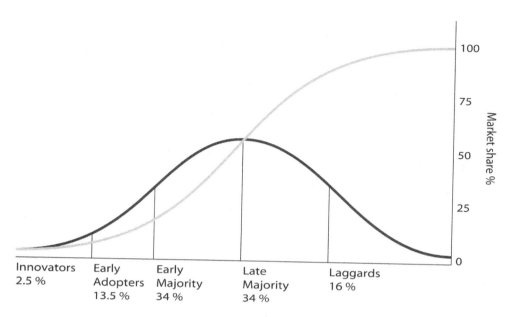

of Innovations. (Note that this illustration of Rogers's idea comes from Wikimedia Commons [http://commons.wikimedia.org/wiki/Main_Page], which is a source of copyright and/or royalty-free images.)

If you have one of the libraries that have the time, money, and staff to be innovators, then you are in rare company and you are doing a great service to the profession. Innovators are experimenters and trailblazers. They try something without knowing whether it will succeed or whether there will be an audience for it. If the innovators develop something that looks promising, then early adopters step in to give it a thorough trail and build an audience. Early adopters are like the scientists who confirm the work of the innovators and find application for it in the real world. Again, it takes time, money, and staff to be an early adopter. The market share of the technology is less than 25 percent even at the end of the early adopter phase.

The early majority phase is characterized by rapid growth in market share, and when the market share hits 50 percent, the late majority phase begins. Laggards adopt the technology only after it has reached 80 percent market penetration and represent the last 16 percent of the people or institutions to adopt the technology. We do not want our libraries to be perceived as behind the curve, however; most of us cannot afford a service that reaches only 5 percent of our customers. Where we fall on the curve depends on our individual conditions.

Technology is tool that we as reference librarians use to serve our customers better. The ultimate goal of reference service has not changed. We will always strive to help our customers find the information they need and prepare them to live in our information society.

Vocabulary

asynchronous	late majority
bleeding edge	leading edge
chat	LISTA
co-browsing	log
early adopters	pushing
early majority	social media
e-mail	synchronous
innovators	text messaging
instant messaging	trailing edge
laggards	

Questions

What do you see as the future of reference services?

What considerations do you need to keep in mind when helping a customer through a text messaging service?

How would you determine which means of providing reference service to discontinue and which of the services mentioned earlier would be your first choice?

How big does the market share for a technology need to be before a library adopts it?

Assignment

Search a database for a library trend or technology. Analyze the number of results found and the time period covered. Determine what phase from Rogers's Diffusion of Innovations the technology is in and describe why this technology is or is not important to libraries. Be sure to defend your position.

Chapter **6**

The Reference Transaction

In this chapter, we examine reference transaction with a focus on the reference interview and a discussion of communication skills.

WHAT IS THE REFERENCE TRANSACTION?

The reference transaction is our opportunity to interact with our customers. It is where we discover the true nature and extent of their information need regardless of the medium in which it takes place. A successful reference transaction requires great skill on the part of the librarian. These skills are often overlooked because of the need to know so many information sources and how to use them. However, these skills are essential to providing reference services and giving the customer a positive user experience.

The elements of the reference transaction, built upon the model by Jesse H. Shera (1976), are outlined in Figure 6.1.

Customer

The customer for school librarians is usually a student but also includes teachers and parents. The customer is the reason the process exists. This book uses the term "customer" to reflect our clientele. Other terms like patron or user have been applied. For our purposes, customer is the best term to use. It reminds us that we are in a customer service profession, and using business terminology reminds us that we are running a business that would not exist without our customers. It also reminds us that we need to treat our customers well, because we need their repeat business. More importantly, as professionals, we want to ensure that we can provide continued assistance to our

Figure 6.1. The Reference Transaction

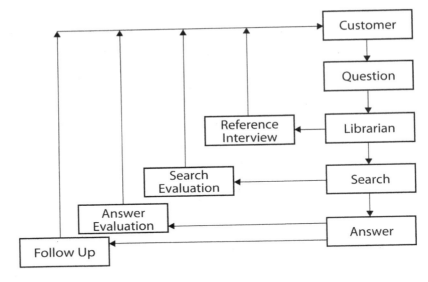

customers to help them meet their information needs and provide information literacy instructions.

Question

The question is the information need and how the customer expresses it. We will discuss this further in the section Reference Interview as it is at this point that the reference interview begins.

There are no stupid questions. Every librarian has heard this motto, and it is illustrative of a professional attitude that librarians should exhibit. If a customer is willing to ask you a question, then you should respect the customer and his or her question and provide him or her the level of service needed in providing an answer to the inquiry.

Librarian

We are the librarian in this model. We interact with both the customer and his or her question. We bring our knowledge of resources and our search skills to help our customers navigate the information world, the context in which information exists. We need to remember that the reference transaction is an interactive process and an evaluative process. We need to evaluate how the process is going, our understanding of the question, the search we conducted, and the results we receive, all the while getting feedback from the customer that impacts the whole process and keeping in mind their age and abilities.

In short, we bring our professionalism to each and every reference transaction regardless of what the question is or who is asking it. We do not judge the customer or his or her need, and we do not censor the information we provide to the customer based on our personal beliefs.

Reference Interview

The reference interview is where we determine the exact nature of the information need. It is during this process that we discover what the customer is really asking and the extent of information needed to answer his or her question. This is the first feedback loop in the reference transaction, a point at which we seek additional input from the customer. This process is also called question negotiation because of the back and forth with the customer as we try to determine the information need. We will expand on this very important step in the section Reference Interview.

Search

The search is what the librarian conducts or guides the customer to conduct to answer his or her question. The librarian must help the customer translate his or her basic question into a valid search strategy. The search should maximize both effectiveness and efficiency. The strategy must take into consideration all of the library's resources, including print, electronic, and the entire learning community, that may be able to answer the question.

This step highlights two of the unique abilities that librarians should possess, knowledge of resources and knowledge of search. These also represent the two major components of the information system. Although there will be others who have more depth of knowledge about resources in a specific subject area, like teachers at your school, they will not possess the breadth of knowledge across disciplines that you have. Your understanding of databases and how search works within them makes you the expert.

However, with the amount of resources available, it is not possible to know every resource. The amount of information available can be overwhelming, and if you feel this way, imagine how overwhelming it must seem to your customers. One thing to remember is that a resource can also be another librarian or teacher at your school.

Teachers and other librarians are great resources. Asking them for help is not a sign of weakness but shows your willingness to work with others and learn from them. Collaboration is an essential ingredient for a successful school library. You need to work with teachers to provide information literacy instructions and resources to students for their projects. It is also a great way to promote library services and collections to teachers. Collaboration with other school libraries or the local public library is a good way to illustrate to students that there is a larger learning community beyond the school library.

Search Evaluation

Search evaluation is the second feedback loop in the reference transaction. At this point, you and your customer evaluate the information you are finding. Have you found the answer? Are you on the right track? If so, then you are well on your way to a successful reference transaction. Or have you missed something? Are the materials not relevant to the need? By asking the customer about the results, you get the feedback you need to understand how well the search is going and what you need to do to modify the search to find other material, if necessary. This is where you evaluate your search strategy for effectiveness and efficiency. You need to evaluate your reference interview as well. Are you not finding the right information, because you missed something in the reference interview? If that is the case, you need to fall back to the reference interview and begin again. Perhaps the question being asked does not have an answer, in which case you need to go back to the reference interview and negotiate a new, modified question.

Answer

The answer is the information we give to the customer to answer his or her information need. Because we care about teaching students information literacy skills, the answer may also be instruction and guidance to help the customer find his or her answer instead of the answer itself.

There are times when we cannot provide an answer or even guide a student to the right resources. We may not have the resources necessary to answer the question, or the question being asked does not have an easy, straightforward answer. In this situation, apologize for not being able to directly find the information and explain to the customer that he or she may have to consult multiple sources and put an answer together. Also let the customer know that you will continue to look for information and you will follow up with them.

Many studies have been done over the years that ask customers if librarians answered their questions. Results of the early studies showed that librarians answered questions correctly 55 percent of the time (Hernon and McClure 1986). This came to be known as the 55% Rule. This was a rather dismal statistic that was around for years. Some researchers felt this statistic could not be accurate, studied the validity of the tests, and did their own research. One of these studies was reported in *Library Journal*, and it found that librarians recommended an accurate resource, or strategy 90 percent of the time (Richardson 2002). Further, Hubbertz (2005) noted that "unobtrusive evaluation does not measure the overall quality of reference service" and that the "55% Rule" is a "spurious generalization." These outcomes dispelled the 55 percent myth and took into consideration that we are not always trying to provide an answer but are trying to produce information-literate students.

There are many factors that influence our ability to provide a correct answer. We have talked about resources and search skills. Our reference policies could also influence the outcome by limiting the amount of time that we can spend with each customer, and that policy may have been put in place because the reference desk is very busy. We cannot give the right answer or provide the perfect search strategy 100 percent of the time. We are human after all. However, we should strive to provide the best service we can given the limits placed upon us by policy and resources.

Answer Evaluation

Answer evaluation is the third feedback loop in the reference transaction. The customer evaluates the guidance or information received from the librarian and decides whether the information answers his or her information need.

Although we may evaluate the answer we provided for our own purposes, it is the opinion of the customer that counts. If the customer believes that he or she has received the right information, then we have a successful reference transaction. If the customer feels that he or she does not have the right information, then the customer needs to ask for more help. We need to watch the customer's body language, listen to the tone of voice, and simply ask if the information answers his or her question. If not, then we need to start over.

As a librarian, you do need to evaluate the answer as well. Do you think the information you provided answered the question, or did you not have the resources to provide a satisfactory answer? Did you help your customer become more information literate? Did you meet the service goals and reference philosophy of your library? The best school media specialists always have in mind their philosophy and goals of reference service and then constantly review their service efforts in regard to those goals.

Follow-Up

Librarians do not have unlimited time to help any one customer. We get one student started, then move on to the next, and try to remember to check back in with the first. Follow-up is an important tool for the librarian to employ, and it is the last feedback loop in the reference transaction. Follow-up is returning to a previous customer whom you may have gotten started on his or her research to see how his or her search is proceeding and to answer any questions that may have arisen in the meantime.

You should encourage your customer to return and ask you any questions that arise after you answer his or her question. In a chat reference transaction, reminding the customer to contact you with additional questions is all you can do. However, in an in-person transaction, you should not wait for the customer to find you. You need to be proactive, find the customer you previously helped, and ask him or her how he or she is doing. Follow-up is an important behavior that shows you care about your customer's success and helps build a positive user experience while allowing you to provide more instruction and making sure that your customer is on the right track.

HELPING CUSTOMERS ASK BETTER QUESTIONS AS PART OF THE REFERENCE INTERVIEW

The second step in the reference transaction, the question, is the point where the reference interview begins. The purpose of the reference interview is to determine the information need of the customer. The question that the customer asked may not reflect what he or she really wants. It does seem odd to assume that the customer does not know what he or she is asking for, but learning to ask good questions takes practice and guidance. Perhaps more importantly, the customer is operating in the information system that may be very unfamiliar to him or her, and the customer does not know how to approach the system and ask meaningful questions within that system.

Many librarians have had a customer come up to the reference desk and ask, "Do you have any books, here?" Behind the librarian in clear view of the customer are stacks of books. In this situation, is the customer really asking if there are any books? Is the proper answer to that question, "Yes"? To understand what the customer really wants, we need to ask them questions that clarify what they really need.

If everyone knew how to ask a really good question, one that perfectly represented his or her information need, the reference interview would not be necessary. Everyone would come up to the reference desk and ask for exactly what he or she needed. We would then provide the answer or help the customer devise a strategy for finding it. Asking good questions seems like a skill that everyone should possess. Like all skills, however, we need to learn how to ask good questions and have the opportunity to practice.

The librarian can help customers by modeling good question-asking skills during the interview process. Another part of the interview process is for the librarian to paraphrase the question back to the customer to make sure that the question was understood. During this process, you can again model creating good questions by improving on what the customer asked without changing the meaning of the question. You can then ask the customer to try out the question by repeating it to you to see if it sounds right to him or her.

THE REFERENCE INTERVIEW

The reference interview is a give-and-take with the customer where the questions you ask and the answers you receive help you determine exactly what the customer needs. You should keep your tone even and polite to encourage the customer to talk to you. Ask open-ended questions to get more information about what the customer is looking for. An open-ended question cannot be answered with a "yes" or "no." This is very similar to the definition of a research question, which is a question that cannot be answered with a "yes" or "no" or answered from a single source. Can you tell me more about your topic? What do you already know about your topic? How much information do you need?

Ask closed-ended questions to focus in on the types of information needed. A closed-ended question can be answered with a "yes" or "no," or single piece of information. Do you want books or journal articles? Do you need background information? Have you tried anything already? Do you need current or historical information? Finally, paraphrase and repeat the question back to the student to make sure you have it right. So you need books about the ecology of the rain forest in South America, preferably with maps and color pictures?

Remember, you are performing the reference interview to make sure you help the customer find exactly what he or she needs and not what you think the customer needs. The purpose of the interview is to help you help the customer. Do not be afraid to ask questions to get to the heart of the matter. It shows interest in the customer's request. It will also result in a more efficient and effective search, a more successful reference transaction, and a better user experience for the customer.

Once you have determined the information need, you need to determine how much help the customer needs in devising a search strategy and choosing a resource to search. For example, if a student asks what the average July high temperature is for Salt Lake City, you could show the student how to find *The*

Weather Almanac in the catalog and have him or her go to the shelf and pull the book. The student can bring the book back to you so you can show how to use it to find his or her answer, and then you can also show the student the other kinds of information *The Weather Almanac* contains. In this encounter, you have made judgments about the student's ability, helped the student find the answer needed, and provided the student with information literacy instruction.

The questions you ask the customer can help him or her become more information literate by helping him or her think through finding his or her own answers. For example, if a student asks for information on cloning his or her dog, you could ask whether he or she thinks that information would be in a book or a journal article and explain the difference. You can also ask the student what he or she already knows about cloning and if the student does not have a good idea of what it is, you can suggest a background source from your reference collection. This is another opportunity to teach information literacy skills, in this case what background information is, and how to use the reference collection, while helping the student find the answer to his or her question.

THE IMPORTANCE OF COMMUNICATION SKILLS

We talked about the RUSA *Guidelines for Behavioral Performance of Reference and Information Service Providers* in Chapter 4 (Reference and User Services Association 2004). It is an invaluable guide to how you can make the reference transaction better by using good communication skills. The first behavior listed in the guidelines is approachability. For the in-person transaction, this guideline deals with nonverbal communication.

We need to be aware of the signals we send to our customers through our body attitudes. For example, arms folded across the chest or staring intently at the computer screen at the reference desk does not send positive, welcoming signals, but quite the opposite, and may keep customers from asking questions. Talking to a customer without making eye contact is another example of bad nonverbal communications. At best, it sends a mixed message that you are willing to help, but only up to point. At worst, it tells the customer that you are not interested in helping him or her at all. We need to appear relaxed, not fidgety or busy. We need to establish eye contact and offer a greeting. We should speak in a calm voice, give our full attention to the customer, and be courteous. Smiling is you best tool. It both welcomes and puts customers at ease.

Our verbal communication skills are important to all mediums we may use in the reference transaction. Whether virtual or in person, we need to use clear, direct language to prevent confusing our customers. The vocabulary we chose should be appropriate to the customers' age levels. If we need to use terminology that may not be understood, then we should explain it.

We need to be aware of the medium we are using when communicating with our customers. We can provide a running narrative as we show a customer how to search a database in person, but we cannot do the same in a chat environment even if it allows for cobrowsing. Typing takes more time than speaking. Another consideration for virtual mediums is the time you take to respond. If you ask the customer to wait while you check for answers, he or she may get impatient waiting for a response or assume that a problem has occurred with the connection and he or she has been dropped. When the customer is waiting, he or she cannot see you working; the customer can only see a screen that is not changing. If you have reached the one-minute mark and have not communicated with the customer, send the customer a quick note to let him or her know you are working on his or her question and will be back shortly. This will let the customer know that you are still there, and he or she will be less likely to disconnect.

It is a good idea to show personality. It is more welcoming and humanizing. Be sure to show the best side of your personality. Humor is perfectly acceptable. There are a few things to remember about humor, however. Everyone has a different sense of humor, and your attempts at being funny may fall flat. Although humor can help you through misunderstandings and mistakes, according to the University of Manitoba via Meghan Harper's (2011) book, sarcasm should be avoided because young children think it is mean and teens find it offensive and degrading.

The reference transaction seems like a simple process: a student asks you a question, and you answer it. But there are many variables and influences involved in the process. First, there are two humans involved who are each bringing their mental and emotional states to the process. The customer may suffer from library anxiety, a fear of asking for help, or not knowing how the information system works. Being a good reference librarian takes more than search skills and knowledge of resources. You need to understand the reference transaction and the reference interview. You need to know why these processes can be intimidating for students. You need to listen carefully, communicate well, and ask appropriate questions. You need a positive service attitude and the willingness to always try your best with all aspects of the reference transaction to help all of your customers with their information needs regardless of the their skill level and the nature of their inquiry. This is professionalism.

EXAMPLE TRANSACTIONS

A student approaches the reference desk and asks: "I need to find something about Martin Luther and his impact on education. Can you help me?"

There are a number of aspects to this questions that you should be able to recognize. First, the question is well stated. You could ask the student how much information he or she needs or what types of information he or she is looking for. A good question to begin with would be, how much do you know about this topic? The word "something" is a good clue that the student does not know much about this subject. If the student tells you that in answer to your question, then you can suggest a background source.

Another aspect of the question is that it has two key ideas: Martin Luther and education. The student needs to find the intersection of these two ideas. This is a classic illustration of the Boolean AND operator that we will examine closely in Chapter 12. You recognize that the question does not require a database search but can be answered from the reference collection. You know this because the question is fairly specific and closed-ended. It is not as broad nor as open-ended as "What impact did the Protestant Reformation have on education?" Even if the student insisted he or she wanted a journal article, you may direct him or her to the reference collection first as a means to activate his or her background knowledge.

Now you are ready to pick a background source from your reference collection to answer the question. Because you know that it is a Boolean search, you will pick a source that covers one of the two ideas and then look for the other in it. This means that you are going to use either an education encyclopedia or a religion encyclopedia. Thinking about the nature of the request, you choose the education encyclopedia. This is the print equivalent of selecting the right database to search. You realize that a religion encyclopedia would have a significant amount of information on Martin Luther. It may mention the impact his ideas had on education, but you would have to shift through a lot of information to find it. You know that going to the education encyclopedia and looking up Martin Luther would show you only the information about Martin Luther that is related to education. You know that this will be an efficient and effective means to answer the questions, because books lend themselves to one topic searches.

A young student approaches you and asks, "Do you have any books on training goldfish?" Off the top of your head, you know that you do not. Do you double check the catalog, tell her no, or ask a clarifying question?

You could make a show of searching the catalog, tell the student you did not find anything, and then suggest searching for journal articles. Your search for journal articles does not find anything that would be useful to him or her. What is your next step?

Or you could ask the student if she is writing a report. The student then tells you that he or she is working on a science fair project. You have a separate section for your science fair books, and you suggest one of those books that give information on creating science fair projects and advise him or her to look through the other sources. You suggest that the student get started looking, and you will check another resource.

You perform a Google search and find a number of videos on YouTube about training goldfish. You go back to your student, tell him or her what you found, and show him or her how you found it. You put him or her on a computer he or she can use to watch the videos. Now you determine if he or she can find them, again, or if he or she will need help. If the student can, you tell him or her you will check back with him or her to see how he or she is doing. If the student cannot find, you help him or her perform the search. In either case, you have helped the student find the information needed and helped develop his or her information literacy skills.

Vocabulary

answer	feedback loop
answer evaluation	follow-up
chat	in-person reference
clarifying question	librarian
closed-ended question	library anxiety
customer	medium
e-mail	nonverbal communication

open-ended question

question

question negotiation

reference interview

search

search evaluation

text messaging

virtual reference

Questions

What does it mean if the customer is dissatisfied and decides not to ask for anymore help?

How do you keep an even tone in a chat transaction?

Name some specific causes of library anxiety? What can be done to alleviate this feeling?

What is a feedback loop and how does it impact the reference transaction?

Assignment

Which step in the reference transaction do you think is the most important for finding the right answer, and which one do you think is the most important to creating a positive user experience? Defend and support your position.

Chapter 7

Reference Resources

This chapter covers the sources you can use to help you identify resources for your reference collection and discusses the medium and types of reference resources available.

IDENTIFYING RESOURCES FOR YOUR REFERENCE COLLECTION

Collection development is the process of identifying, selecting, weeding, and acquiring resources for your library. When it comes to purchasing resources, we need to make sure that we are buying resources that are of high quality and represent good value. Identifying these resources is an important part of the job.

Fortunately, there are many resources designed to help you find the materials you need for your library. Publishers are happy to send you catalogs and make their catalogs available through their Web sites. A publisher's catalog is not the best resource for identifying specific items for your collection. You cannot expect a fair and an unbiased review from the publisher, but it will at least show you what is available and how much it will cost. This can be used to compare one resource to another.

You can make purchasing decisions based on a publisher's catalog alone, but you have to be very confident in the quality of materials that the publisher produces. In this regard, it helps if you have purchased resources from this publisher before, so that you have already evaluated its products. However, a reputable publisher is no guarantee of quality resources that meet your needs. Unless you really need a resource for that subject area or cannot find any other resource for that subject, you may want to delay a purchase decision until you are able to read reviews of the resource.

Reviews are of paramount importance in helping you select resources. Professional publications, like *School Library Journal* and *Booklist*, will review reference resources in addition to fiction and informational sources. *Library Journal* and *Choice* also review reference resources, but with an emphasis on public and academic library resources, respectively. Then there are the bibliographies. These sources gather or create reviews of resources that are linked together by the theme or subject of the parent sources. For example, *Children's Catalog* and *Children's Core Collection* list good fiction and informational resources for your library, with the former being a print resource and the latter being available as a print or an electronic resource.

Professional reviews handle the quality analysis of the resources. They let you know if the resource is good, bad, or indifferent and will best serve the audience. What they cannot tell you is whether that resource will be a good value for your library.

IS PRINT DEAD?

The media available for reference resources are print and electronic. Electronic reference resources have gained in popularity. They offer some important advantages over print resources. Electronic has grown in popularity at the expense of print. For example, in 2010, academic libraries spent 21 percent of the book and journals backlist money on electronic resources and spent 70 percent of their current journal subscription money on electronic resources (Phan et al. 2011). Print materials still comprised 87.3 percent of public library collections in 2009, but that is down from 93.4 percent in 2000 (Bogart 2012). A study conducted by the Pew Research Center found that 25 percent of Americans between the ages of 16 and 29 had read an e-book in 2012. It also reported 75 percent of that age group had reported reading a print book in that same year (Zickuhr, Rainie, and Purcell 2013).

A statistic that illustrates what percentage of the reference budget is spent on electronic sources was not found. Public libraries, however, did spend more than $48 million on electronic references resources in 2010, which represents about 6¾ percent of their total acquisitions budget, and academic libraries spent $147.5 million, or nearly 13¾ percent of their acquisitions budget on these resources (Bogart 2012). The numbers do indicate the importance of electronic reference resources to reference collections.

The statistics are a good indication that print is not dead. A more relevant question for this text would be: Is print, as far as reference resources go, a dead medium? That is a more difficult question to answer. The numbers show significant expenditures on electronic reference, and personal experience confirms this. Is there any reason to buy print reference resources?

PRINT RESOURCES

Print reference resources have a few advantages over the electronic counterparts for your customers and for your teaching needs. First, they are easy to use. Good print resources work well for their intended audience. They are easier to use and understand for younger customers. They offer a simple browsibility that electronic sources cannot match. They serve as a good introduction to databases, because the information contained within them is structured like a database. They also serve as a good, simplified introduction to searching with a table of contents that leads you to chapters, broad categories of information, and an index that takes you to specific pieces of information.

From a collection development perspective, print reference books offer a few other advantages. First, there are still more of them. While there are many reference books that have an electronic counterpart, you are still more likely to find a book on a specific topic than a database. You can control your costs better with print sources. You buy a reference book once. You do not get charged for it again the next year and at a higher rate than you paid before. You can choose when and if to update your print source. For example, you buy *The World Book Encyclopedia* one year. If you want, you can buy the updated version the very next year, or you can choose to wait a number of years before updating it.

Print generally costs less. Electronic resources charge a premium over their print counterparts for the format, searchability, and access. In addition, there is often a hosting fee, which is a charge for providing access to the resource that has to be paid annually. Cost per use, a number you calculate by taking the initial cost of the resource and dividing it by the number of times it got used, often favors print especially for lower-use resources. The lower the cost per use, the greater the value received from the resource.

ELECTRONIC RESOURCES

Electronic reference resources have their advantages too. They are easy to search, though not easy to search well. Google has made them familiar to everyone. Type any term in to the search box, and they will find something. They are fast and efficient. They can search vast quantities of information in a fraction of a second. This fact alone has upended the research process.

Electronic resources allow multiple points of seamless access to the information they contain. A print resource has to have multiple indexes or an extensive index to provide somewhat similar access, and the more and bigger the indexes it has, the more difficult it becomes to use. Electronic resources support multiple users simultaneously, while a book is generally one volume, one user. Electronic resources support remote access. Customers do not have to be in the library to use the resource. This makes your collections available to your students whenever they want to use them and wherever they happen to be.

Electronic resources can be a great value, with an extremely low cost per use. As electronic resources become the go to resources in your library, their use goes up, and their cost per use goes down. They can be purchased by a consortium of libraries to lower the costs and serve a larger audience. Your school district or your state may purchase these resources and make them available to everyone in their respective audiences while not taking any of your budget.

There are two broad categories of electronic reference resources. The first represents a single source like the *Encyclopaedia Britannica* or *Chemical Elements* published by UXL. For the purposes of this book, we will refer to these sources as e-books. The second category of electronic resources is databases.

Databases aggregate many sources into one place. Databases can consist of thousands of journals, hundreds of e-books, photos, primary documents, music, and anything else that can be digitized. *MAS Ultra* is an example of a database aimed at high school students that incorporates many kinds of resources. *Gale Virtual Reference Library* allows you to purchase individual e-books and access and search them all at once or individually.

TYPES OF REFERENCE RESOURCES

With the exception of databases, there are seven types of reference resources. They are divided by the kinds of information they contain. The types are:

- Almanacs, Yearbooks, and Handbooks
- Atlases and Gazetteers
- Bibliographies
- Biographies
- Dictionaries
- Directories
- Encyclopedias

Almanacs, Yearbooks, and Handbooks

Almanacs are typically full of short, factual entries, like lists of the presidents and World Series winners. Almanacs use tables and lists to present a lot of information in a small amount of space. Coverage is extremely broad but lacks any depth, but where else would you find the most popular breeds of cats in the same place as the population of Turkey and Olympic records? The information is both historical and current. To keep the information current, print almanacs are updated yearly and are contained within one volume. *The World Almanac and Book of Facts* is a classic almanac that has been published since 1868 ("The World Almanac and Book of Facts" 2013). Almanacs are the best choice for quick facts and figures.

Yearbooks fall into the same category as almanacs. They differ from almanacs in that they contain current information only. Yearbooks may have broad coverage or may focus on a specific discipline. *Guinness World Records* is a yearbook. It is published annually and contains only the current world records. There are no lists of past records and their holders.

Handbooks are placed into this category because their entries are relatively short. Handbooks try to give a comprehensive overview of a topic in one volume. The topic can be broad like American literature or more narrowly focused like Herman Melville. In any case, the result is a book with breadth and little depth. Publishing schedules vary. Most handbooks do not contain the type of information that needs to be updated annually. The Oxford Companions are classic examples of handbooks. They are one-volume overviews of a topic with necessarily short entries. The more important the topic of the entry is to the work, the longer the entry will be. Longer entries are often signed or initialed by their authors and have a short bibliography or a list of further readings.

Atlases and Gazetteers

Atlases are geographic representations of information. *The Rand McNally Road Atlas* is an example of an atlas that most of us know with its graphic depiction of interstates, highways, county roads, and even city streets. *National Geographic Concise Atlas of the World* has maps that show political boundaries, borders of states and countries, physical features like mountain ranges, rivers, and forests, and thematic maps that show such things as distribution of populations and religions. Historical atlases have political and thematic maps that show such things as battle fields and troop movements during the Revolutionary War.

Gazetteers contain geographic information, but no maps showing that information. Gazetteers are an alphabetical list of cities, mountains, rivers, parks, and states. The information frequently includes location, specifically longitude and latitude, elevation, population, and history of the place name. An example of a gazetteer is *The Columbia Gazetteer of the World*. It is a large three-volume set, and like all gazetteers, it is a very specialized resource. It will not get the same amount of use as an atlas, but it can answer some geographic questions quickly and easily.

Bibliographies

Bibliographies are lists of resources in any medium that are thematically linked. Bibliographies are the original research tool and were the only research tool for hundreds of years ("The Earliest Surviving Detailed Bibliographical Entries" 2013). What we think of as the traditional bibliography, lists of books, has declined in importance as other search tools developed to provide access to new information resources, like journals and journal indexes.

At the beginning of this chapter, two bibliographic sources were mentioned as aids to selection, *Children's Catalog* and *Children's Core Collection*. The theme that links the sources together within the bibliography is good books for elementary school children. That is a broad thematic link. The thematic link may be broad or narrow. A bibliography can list all the works of one individual author as they appear in any medium like *The Dr. Seuss Catalog* or list the important publications in all disciplines of psychology in the previous year like *Annual Review of Psychology*. Bibliographies can simply list sources or can also contain annotations. An annotated bibliography includes a short, critical summary of the listed resources or a review.

Finally, bibliographies as we know them today are our most important research tools: databases. A database is a list of thematically linked resources in any medium. The theme is very broad. For *Academic Search Premier*, the theme is journal sources that are suitable for academic research. The advantages these electronic bibliographies have over their print counterparts are their searchability and the presence of the item to which it refers. Full-text databases are the modern, improved version of the bibliography.

Biographies

Biographic resources in the reference collection serve a different purpose than book-length biographies in the circulating collection. The reference resources are designed to provide quick overviews or quick facts. For example, *Almanac of Famous People* provides birth dates, death dates if the person is dead, occupation, and one sentence that tells why the person is famous. A resource like *Current Biography* gives you a short three- or four-page biography of a notable, living person.

Who's Who in America is another resource for famous people, but in this case they must be living Americans. *Who's Who* includes only a paragraph or two of information, and the information is provided by the subject. Contact information is also supplied for the person in question. *Dictionary of American Biography* takes a very different approach. While it includes only famous Americans like *Who's Who*, none of the people are living, and the biographies are multiple pages long and written by scholars.

Scope, depth, and breadth vary widely for biographical sources. Consider what types of biographical information you need to support the questions you receive from your customers. One resource will probably not be able to handle the majority of the questions you receive. So you will need to consider multiple resources that suit your needs.

Dictionaries

Dictionaries are a broader category of resources than one would assume. We all know what a dictionary is, and it does not seem like there would be a lot of variety in dictionaries. But there is. The distinction is between abridged and unabridged dictionaries. *Merriam-Webster's Collegiate Dictionary* is a well-known example of an abridged dictionary. An abridged dictionary does not try to define all the words in a language, but tries to include the most commonly used words. *Merriam-Webster's Collegiate Dictionary* contains 225,000 definitions, not entries (Merriam-Webster, Inc. 2010a). This certainly seems like a very large number, but *Webster's Third New International Dictionary, Unabridged*, defines more than 476,000 entries (Merriam-Webster, Inc. 2010b). Note the difference in descriptions.

Dictionaries may be descriptive or prescriptive. A descriptive dictionary describes the language as currently spoken and used. A prescriptive dictionary will tell you the preferred pronunciation and use. Cobuild dictionaries like *Collins COBUILD School Dictionary of American English* use the word in context in a full sentence to show the proper, contemporary usage of the word. The *Oxford English Dictionary* also uses quotes to illustrate word usage. The difference is that the quotes in the *Oxford English Dictionary* are historical in nature and show the first use of a meaning of the word in context. Combined with more than 600,000 definitions of words, this makes the *Oxford English Dictionary* the resource for etymological information ("Oxford English Dictionary" 2013).

The dictionaries discussed earlier are all general dictionaries. There are subject-specific dictionaries that focus on the language of a particular profession or field of study. *The AMA Dictionary of Business and Management* and *A Dictionary of Ecology* are two examples of subject-specific dictionaries. The definitions for words in subject-specific dictionaries will pertain only to that subject, even if the word has many other meanings beyond that discipline.

Dictionaries are available for students of all levels, from visual dictionaries for the very young through collegiate and unabridged dictionaries. They are invaluable resources. You need to have a selection of dictionaries to satisfy your customers' needs.

Directories

The phone book is the classic example of a directory. If you need a phone number, you grab the phone book and look it up. What if you need the chief financial officer of Apple Computer or the address of the Deltiologists of America? You use directories like *Standard and Poor's Register* and the *Encyclopedia of Associations* to find your answers.

Directories contain contact information like name, address, phone number, and Web address. Depending on the subject of the directory, other information will also be included. *Writer's Market* is a directory. It lists contact information of many publications, but in addition to that, it also contains submission guidelines and types of articles accepted by those publications. *College Blue Book* lists the admission requirements and the programs of study at colleges and universities across the country, including the contact information. *The United States Government Manual* gives contact information of federal departments and also outlines the functions of those departments.

Directory information dates quickly. Access to the Internet may be more important than the contact information supplied by directories. However, because many of these directories offer other kinds of information, you need to evaluate the need for the type of information provided by the specific directory you are considering. A high school library needs something like *College Blue Book* to support its students. A print edition may not need to be updated every year because the information on admissions and programs does not change rapidly, and the contact can be checked on the Internet.

Encyclopedias

General encyclopedias have a difficult job. They try to cover the world of knowledge by including every major subject area from painting to space exploration, from dogs to cats, and from fission to jazz fusion. General encyclopedias are written for different audiences. *The World Book Encyclopedia* is intended for elementary through middle school children. *Encyclopedia Americana* is written for middle school through high school and even undergraduates. *Encyclopaedia Britannica's* audience is high school students, undergraduates, and adults.

Specialized or subject-specific encyclopedias have a narrower scope and therefore can provide greater depth of coverage while providing complete coverage of their subject. Some subjects are broader than others. *The McGraw-Hill Encyclopedia of Science & Technology* has a broader scope than the *Gale Encyclopedia of Childhood and Adolescence*. As with general encyclopedias, subject encyclopedias can be one volume or many volumes. *The Dictionary of Art* runs 34 volumes, and the *Encyclopedia of Volcanoes* is one volume.

Articles in encyclopedias have more depth than most other reference sources because they have more length than most reference sources. With the exception of the shortest articles, articles are often signed or initialed by their authors, and short bibliographies are often included. Most general encyclopedias update their print editions yearly. However, they update only some of the articles for each new edition. The Web versions of these resources offer faster updates, additional materials, media, and links to other resources. It is such a good method for delivering information that *Encyclopaedia Britannica* has stopped publishing its print edition after a 244-year publishing history (Britannica Editors 2012).

This is the Wikipedia model, and no discussion of encyclopedias would be complete without mentioning Wikipedia. Wikipedia (http://www.wikipedia .org) has changed our understanding of what an encyclopedia is. It is loved by some and hated by others. However, as one of the most popular Web sites, your students have used it; therefore, you should too. No encyclopedia is as big as the Wikipedia. The Wikipedia has 4.289 million articles in the English language ("Main Page" 2013), whereas the *Encyclopaedia Britannica Online* has 120,000 entries ("Wikipedia:Size Comparisons" 2013). Wikipedia has had an image problem related to its accuracy. However, there are many studies that show the accuracy of Wikipedia articles ("Reliability of Wikipedia" 2013). Do note that the citation in the previous sentence is to a Wikipedia article. An article from LiveScience attests to the accuracy of that Wikipedia page and points out a few interesting issues it uncovered with Wikipedia (Wolchover 2013).

Wikipedia presents a good teaching opportunity. You can stress to your students the importance of confirming the information they find in one source by checking it against another source whether they find the information in Wikipedia or elsewhere.

Vocabulary

almanacs	directories
annotated bibliography	e-books
atlases	encyclopedias
bibliographies	gazetteers
biographies	handbooks
browsibility	index
collection development	reviews
cost per use	searchability
databases	table of contents
dictionaries	

Questions

How is cost per use reflected in decisions to purchase resources?

What are your feelings about the death of print resources or print reference resources?

Did *Encyclopaedia Britannica* make the right decision to stop publishing its print edition? Why or why not?

Is there any need to have print directories in reference collections?

What are your feelings about Wikipedia?

If you could have only one dictionary for your library, which one would it be and why?

Assignment

Find a print and an electronic resource from the same type of reference resources (dictionaries, encyclopedias, etc.), evaluate them, and compare them to each other. Which one is easiest to use? Which one has more information? Which one is the better resource and why?

Other than the resources already listed, find two other resources of each type, either print or electronic, and create an annotated bibliography.

Chapter **8**

Evaluating Information and Resources

This chapter examines the process of evaluating information and the resources that contain it. We discuss why it is important for you and your students to know how to evaluate resources. Finally, we provide an evaluation checklist to make the process easier.

ELEMENTS OF EVALUATION

School librarians need to be experts at evaluating information and information resources. We need to be able to select the best resources for our libraries with our limited budgets. On the other hand, we must also be able to teach our students how to evaluate information to meet our curricular goals and to give students one of the most important skills they will need to make good decisions throughout their personal and professional lives.

In a study for Project Information Literacy, the authors found that 61 percent of the college students interviewed turned to friends and family when they needed help evaluating information, 49 percent turned to their instructors, and 11 percent turned to the librarian (Head and Eisenberg 2010b). Clearly, students need help evaluating resources, and just as obviously, we need to do a better job teaching students how to evaluate resources and letting them know that we are their ally in this cause.

Identifying good, valid, and useful information from the overwhelming amounts available is an essential information literacy skill. To help with the evaluation process, we will divide it into five elements. The first three may be applied by you or your customers in evaluating the information found. The last two are aimed specifically at the needs of the school library. The five elements of evaluation are:

- Relevance
- Purpose
- Validity
- Usability
- Cost

There is no agreement on the terminology, or number of elements in the evaluation process. You will encounter variations, but the purpose is the same: to give you a framework from which to evaluate information, and information resources.

Relevance

Relevance is the easiest of the evaluation criteria to learn and apply. Relevance is determining if the information you found is relevant to your research paper or project or whether the resource is relevant to the needs of your customers. Students can find a lot of information very quickly, and once they have, they need to ask, is that information relevant? Does it help me answer my information need? Does it address the research question I proposed or the hypothesis I stated. If not, is it a negative example that helps prove my point, or does it just need to be discarded?

As a school librarian, the questions are broader, but the answers reflect the same point. Does this resource fill a need in my collection? Will it support the curriculum? Will my students use it? Relevance is the first cut. Whatever information or resources that survive this step should relate to the topic, question, or need being addressed. They should have relevance. From here, a more in-depth analysis can begin.

Purpose

The purpose of the information or resource encompasses its type, scope, and style. Resource types reflect the nature of the material. There are three basic types of resources. Primary research is associated with scholarly journal articles. Primary research is done by scientists and professors in all disciplines, and its purpose is to uncover or discover new insights or all together new information. Not every article in a scholarly journal is a primary research article. Scholarly journals contain editorials, letters to the editor, news items, and reviews in addition to primary research. It is important to be able to distinguish the research article from the other material in a scholarly journal. Primary research is often very structured. It will state the hypothesis, the methodology used to test it, the outcomes, and conclusions drawn from the research, along with a bibliography. It may also contain a literature review, a survey of related articles in the discipline, graphs, and tables. To incorporate all this information, primary research articles are often long.

A primary source is a source that is directly related to a person or a time period. Primary sources illuminate people or events from a personal perspective. They are firsthand accounts of events from people who were involved in them or documents and materials these people produced. For example, if you were studying the Great Depression, then primary sources would be letters, diaries, newspapers, photographs and other documents produced during that period in history. If you were studying President Franklin D. Roosevelt, then a collection of FDR's correspondence would be a primary source of information about him.

Secondary sources are not primary. They incorporate primary research and primary sources, but they are not engaged in finding new information. They gather and summarize information as it currently exists. A biography is an example of a secondary source, whereas an autobiography is a primary source. An encyclopedia article is another example of a secondary source. There will be no original research in an encyclopedia article. Instead, you will find a synthesis of current thinking and well-established information selected and arranged to give you an overview of the subject.

Scope   Scope is what is covered or included in the information or resource. Just as important, scope is also what is not covered and excluded from the resource. Scope reflects the creator's conscious decision on what will and what will not be the focus of the resource. Scope consists of the breadth of coverage and depth of the information provided in the item. A primary research article in a journal may have a very narrow breadth of coverage. Its depth, however, may be very deep. In general, great breadth in a resource means little depth, whereas great depth dictates a narrowly focused breadth. A resource that has both great breadth and depth would also by necessity have great length. Encyclopedias are as close to having both breadth and depth as resources come, but a book on any one topic found within an encyclopedia will have greater depth than an encyclopedia can muster.

As an example, we have four authors who wrote four different books about the Civil War. Each author had to decide what the scope of his or her work would be. The first example work is called *Famous Battles of the Civil War*. The first question you should ask about this resource is what criteria did the author use to determine what qualifies as a famous battle? What battles are excluded and why? What kinds and amounts of information are given for the battles? These questions will help you determine the scope of this resource.

The second example is a book called *A History of the Civil War*. You would expect this book to cover all aspects of the Civil War, and the preface of the book says that it does cover political, military, social, and economic aspects. This particular book is only 150 pages long. With such a broad scope and so few pages, how much depth can this resource offer? Is it enough depth to answer the questions your students might have?

The third book in this example is titled *Letters Home from the Civil War*. It consists entirely of letters from soldiers on both sides of the conflict written to their families. The letters are arranged in chronological order. What types of questions will this resource be able to answer? Will it contain detailed battle plans, or discussions of the political aspects of the war?

The fourth and final book is called *Life During the Civil War*. It covers what daily life on the home front was like during the time of the Civil War. It talks about wages, working conditions, what a typical home looked like, how it was furnished at various class levels, social norms, and religious and political beliefs. Although it is a good book like the others, it makes no mention of any battles, does not talk about what the political leaders were trying to do, and does not use real people as examples. This book shows how people lived during the time of the Civil War. It will answer a different set of questions than any of the other resources. It still needs to answer the question, is this relevant? These differences between the books in this example come down to scope, the breadth, and depth of coverage.

For students, the question of scope comes down to, does this information resource answer my question? Is there too little or too much information, or does it match the scope of my project? Is there is a big mismatch between the scope of the resource and the scope of my project? Is there information I can use, and will I be able to extract that information easily from that source? This is scope and why it is important.

Style   Style is the author's choice of words in the broadest sense. Style is how the author writes, his or her tone of voice, the intended audience, and his or her point of view. Style is much more strongly associated with fiction, even informational books than it is with reference materials. However, style has a strong impact on the evaluation of information and information resources. Imagine a dictionary that defines a word by using that word in the definition, by using at least three more words that you need to look up to understand the definition, by being so vague that the definition is meaningless, or by taking a paragraph to say what should be said in a short sentence. Dictionary definitions need clear, direct writing that their intended audience can understand. This is a function of style.

Reference resources should present their material in a straightforward, even-handed manner, but the tone of voice can differ. Most reference resources have a formal, scholarly tone of voice. A few have an informal, conversational tone. The intended audience of the material affects its style and tone of voice. A book written for sixth graders will not have the same vocabulary or tone as a book written for college students. What is considered scholarly sounding to a sixth grader is very different from what sounds scholarly to a college student. The style, how the information is conveyed, needs to be appropriate for the intended audience.

Point of view is generally to be avoided in reference material, but it is the hallmark of fiction and important to informational resources as well. Point of view is the perspective that the author brings to the material or even imposes on the material. Point of view can range from an even-handed presentation of all sides of an issue, or a presentation of the facts of a research study, to blatant propaganda that tries to convince its audience of the rightness of its opinions in the absence of facts. The authors of a reference or an informational resource should not be trying to sell you their religious, political, personal, or scientific opinions. They should be presenting the facts as supported by valid research. A book with a scholarly tone can be trying to convince you that cigarettes do not cause cancer. Tone of voice should not influence the interpretation of a resource's validity, nor should it mask a resource's point of view.

Point of view often leads to questions of validity. If you encounter an article that has a strong point of view, then it is extremely important that the validity of the source be examined. Students need to learn about bias, how it is reflected in the point of view or an information source, and how it destroys the validity of a source. Students will often use editorials from newspapers or scholarly journals in their reports because they do not understand that an editorial is an opinion piece that may have no supporting evidence. The Web presents even more problems. Students can scoop up large amounts of information that may look good but have a strong bias and misrepresented facts. Students need to be able to spot snake oil salesmen and how to confirm information by checking other resources.

Validity

Validity is the most difficult of the elements of evaluation for people to understand. It is difficult for us to accept that there are people who are knowingly trying to deceive us, who are willing to tell half-truths, and who manipulate data to support their desired outcomes. Cases like this can be difficult to spot. So how do you spot a case where the author simply overstates his or her conclusion or uses poor resources to support his or her hypothesis? This is why validity is so difficult and so important to the evaluation process.

Validity is the factualness of a resource. Validity consists of three parts that interact and overlap with each other to build the whole picture of a resource's worth. The components of validity are:

- Timeliness
- Accuracy
- Authority

These three components of validity will help you select good resources for students and your library. They are also essential ideas for students to understand, and know how to use when evaluating information, and information resources. With the amount of information available today and the dominance of the Web as a research tool, students are likely to find questionable and inaccurate information. Understanding these principles, and knowing how to apply them will help students select better resources to answer their information needs.

Timeliness   If a reference item is weak in any one of these three areas, it is a good idea to find a different reference source. Print encyclopedias, for example, are often discarded after five years because their information is dated and no longer accurate.

Timeliness is the easiest of the three components to evaluate. Timeliness asks how current the information is. However, it is more than just that. Timeliness also asks how current the sources used in the information resource are. A resource about the solar system could have been published yesterday. That would make it very timely, but if the information used in that resource all came from 50-year-old sources of information, then the information in our new resource is not timely in nature. In fact, it is dated and inaccurate.

Timeliness is important, but it is more important to some disciplines than to others. For some disciplines, like the sciences, the timeliness or currency of the information is of vital importance. New discoveries are happening all the time. Information dates quickly. For other disciplines, the age of the material is not as important as the quality of the material. If you were writing a paper on Shakespeare, you can find lots of great information that is still valid even though it may be many years old. If you were writing about health issues, anything older than five years could be dangerously out of date.

Timeliness is easy to ascertain. You check the publication date. Keep in mind the publication process has an effect on timeliness. The newest information in a book published this year may be at least one year old. That article on the latest discovery may have taken four months to get published in a journal. A Web page may have been updated a week ago or three years ago. Next, check the publication dates of the cited sources. This is how you avoid the trap of a new resource that is using old information.

Accuracy   Accuracy is the veracity of the information presented. It was a long-standing fact that Mount Everest was 29,028′ tall. The height of the mountain was taken recently with modern GPS equipment. It is now a fact that Mount Everest is 29,035′ tall (Brunner 2008). Anything that gives the first number is wrong and therefore inaccurate. This is a simple example, but it does illustrate how difficult it can be to know if the information being presented is correct or not.

One way to check is to compare what two or more resources say about the same thing. If there is agreement, then the source in question is accurate. It is a daunting task to evaluate the accuracy of a reference source that contains thousands of facts. We often rely on reviews to provide us with this information. When looking at a journal article or a Web site, you and your customers will have the same problem: evaluating the accuracy of the resource. Even on this smaller scale, it is still a daunting task. The solution is the same: find another resource that says the same thing. You do not have to check every fact in the article, but check the ones you want to use in your research. Even young students can and should be taught to use more than one resource for their projects or papers.

We mentioned using the references in an information resource to help evaluate its timeliness. Reference can also be examined to help evaluate a resource's accuracy. Which do you think may be more accurate, the 500-page book with a 15-item bibliography or a 200-page book with a 50-item bibliography? Quantity is helpful, but which article would you recommend to a student: the one with 10 citations or the one with 10 citations where 5 of them are to other works by the author of the article being examined? You also need to look at the items in the bibliography and judge their quality. If the article you are reading is a research paper but the items it cites are all from newspapers, news magazines, and the Web, then you should question the accuracy of the article.

Authority   Judging the accuracy of a resource can be difficult and time consuming. It is why we also use authority to judge the validity of resources. We look at the reputation of the publisher and the credentials of the author. These things speak to the authority of the research. Authority is who wrote the material, what his or her qualifications are, and what else he or she has published. Authority is also the references the author chose to support his or her research. Authority is who published the material, what his or her reputation is, what other resources he or she published in the same discipline, and the review process the material underwent before its publication.

When evaluating the authority of an author, check the resource for his or her credentials. For a newspaper article, there may be no credentials listed beyond staff writer. There may be no author listed at all for the article. This is normal. The reporting of the news does not necessarily require credentials of any kind. However, if a Web site purports to have a solution to world poverty, then an author with relevant credentials needs to be listed to give the information credibility. For example, most reference books and primary research articles are written by PhDs. This levels the playing field to some extent. All the authors have some authority. But what if that article on child psychology was written by a person with a PhD in economics? This article would have less authority than those written by experts in the field.

In large reference sources like encyclopedias, the articles are written by many different people. Is each article signed by the person who wrote it, and what are that person's qualifications? Are all the contributors, the authors of the individual articles, listed somewhere in the resource? Are their credentials listed there as well?

Books and journals often list the credentials of their authors. It is a selling point. Web sites, on the other hand, may not provide any information about the author. Should you trust the information from such a site? What is the difference between a .com, .edu, .gov, and .org site (commercial, education, government, and nonprofit organization)? Does that necessarily affect the quality of the information?

What else have the authors written? This is easy to check in commercial databases. You click on an author's name and pull up a list of items by that author in that database. Has the author written many other articles? Have the author's works been well reviewed? Have the author's works been cited by others? It may be hard to find a review of that material. If you have access to a citation database, you can see if an author has been cited by other authors. Very few of us have access to citation databases because they are expensive. However, databases like Academic Search Premier are now including a "Times Cited in This Database" link that gives you some of the same effect as a citation database which is a measure of popularity and impact of an article.

We know that the currency of the references cited affects the overall currency of the item. We know that having appropriate references affects the item's accuracy. Combine these two and add quality references and you have authority. So what are the cited sources? Where are they from? Do they represent the best thinking? Does the author cite only books or only journals? Are they reputable journals and well-reviewed books? Who published the materials? How many citations are there? Does that seem like a lot or a few given the material? You need to look at the references because it will help you understand the author's intent, which we already talked about in the section Style. It will also help you understand the currency and quality of thinking that went into the item.

The publisher is the other piece of the authority puzzle that should be considered when evaluating materials. A reputable publisher is no guarantee of a quality product. However, you are more likely to get a good book, journal, or Web site from a quality publisher than from a lower-tier publisher. A publisher with a reputation for publishing quality resources has earned that reputation through careful selection of resources and good reviews received by those resources. They are unlikely to jeopardize that reputation by publishing something of questionable quality.

You need a book to fill a hole in your reference collection. You have two fliers on your desk for just such a book. One is from Oxford University Press, and the other is self-published by the author. Both books are brand new. There are no reviews, and you need one as soon as possible because an assignment is coming up that will require students to use this resource. Which one would you order sight unseen? Both books might be good, but at least with the book from Oxford University Press, you know it will not be bad.

Scholarly journals subject the articles that are submitted for possible publication to a process known as peer review. Peer review involves a number of experts in the field who review the submissions for quality and worthiness to be published. An article that passes this process has met at least one quality standard already. Publishers of other types of information also have editors and review processes, but these are not of the level and reputation of the peer review process.

The publisher of a Web site can be any individual who wrote and created the whole site, or it can be any organization or group. For some Web sites, it is very clear who the organization or publisher is behind the site. They are recognizable brand names like Wikipedia and WebMD. For other sites, you may have to look closely at the page to determine who the publisher is. Also consider the domain the Web site is a part of when thinking about the publisher. A .com can be a site created by anyone or any for-profit business, and the quality can vary wildly from nonexistent to wonderful. A .org is frequently a nonprofit organization that may provide excellent information or may have a very specific point of view on its topic. Our government collects and publishes vast quantities of data. A government Web site, .gov, can provide statistical data for all subject areas and disciplines. Finally, a .edu can represent a university, its researchers, and scholarship, but it may also be a student Web site that needs to be evaluated closely.

Usability

The last two elements of evaluation are not for students to use when evaluating information, but they are intended for you to use in addition to the other elements when evaluating resources to purchase for your collection. The first of these elements is usability. Usability is how well designed the resource is. Usability consists of two factors. They are format and arrangement.

Format   Format is the physical presence of the resource and includes the layout of information on the page or on the screen. For an illustration of format, take one volume of two different encyclopedias off the shelf, a volume of *Encyclopedia Americana* and *The World Book Encyclopedia*, and then compare them. Start by examining the size of each volume—height, width, and depth. Which one is thicker, taller, and deeper?

Now, open each volume and look at how the material is presented on the page. How many columns of text are there? What font is being used? How large is it? How much white space is there? Are there illustrations, pictures, charts, or drawings? Are they in color or black and white? How thick is the paper stock? Is it glossy or dull? How are text and illustrations laid out? Do they work well together?

Do all of these elements help you find, use, or read the information in the article? Is the format of one encyclopedia better than another? Is the format better for one age group than for another? These are questions of format, the physical presentation of information.

Now take any one of your print encyclopedia volumes and then compare it to any Web-based encyclopedia you have access to. Ask all the same questions of the electronic encyclopedia as you did of the print one. In addition, how are links displayed in the electronic version? Where are additional sources listed on the display? Are all the questions valid for the electronic source? Are there other questions you could ask about the physical presentation of the information that are applicable only to the electronic version? When you compare the two, which one do you think has the better format?

Is the format of a resource important to a student doing a research paper or project? Illustrations may be particularly important to younger students. Size, portability, and other physical factors may play a role in the selection of a resource by a student. However, it is the information that students are seeking, and if it is good, then these basic issues of format are less important. Of course, you need to keep format in mind when considering materials for purchase.

Format is not the same as arrangement. They are often confused for each other because the words in general have similar meanings. However, our definitions are very different. Format is physical. It is how the item looks. Arrangement is intellectual. It is how the information is placed and accessed within the item. They are both important to a good resource but in very different ways. Arrangement is the second piece of the usability puzzle.

Arrangement   Arrangement, as stated earlier, is the intellectual design of the information within the item. This includes all the means provided to access the information. There are many possible arrangements for each type of reference source. Some arrangements work better than others for various types of material. For example, an atlas could arrange its maps by name of country, by population, or by continent. Atlases do not use the first two options. The last choice is how atlases arrange the maps. This is clearly a better intellectual design of the information in an atlas.

Using our fictitious *Famous Battles of the Civil War* as an example, we can arrange the material in a number of different ways. Our book could arrange the battles geographically, chronologically, by generals involved, by state where they took place, or by importance. A print reference source can arrange the material in the book only in one permanent way; this includes the main body of the work, the informational heart of the book, the table of contents, and the index. The author must choose which arrangement the print source will have. An electronic version of this book may offer many ways to move through the information and allow you to choose the method that appeals to you the most, like chronological by general. In print sources, tables of contents are created to show the arrangement of information and to provide a means of jumping into the text. Indexes are created to give points of access to specific pieces of information, and cross-references are used to guide you to the proper index term. Our Civil War book could choose to arrange the main body of the work chronologically and then provide an index that lists generals, locations, companies, casualties, and so on.

When looking at a single entry in a reference resource, examine the logic behind the presentation of the information. Does it make sense? Will students be able to use this resource easily? Does the information flow in a logical manner?

Look for the standard features that are included in each entry in a reference resource. Does each article have a history of the topic and a summary of the current state of affairs? Is there a pronunciation guide or an actual pronunciation? Is each article signed by an author? Is there a link from the author's name to other items written by that author or information about that author? Is there a list of further readings or some sort of bibliography, and are there links to these resources? Are these features fillers, or do they help you use the work and understand the information?

The arrangement of the information provides points of access. In a print resource, the main body provides one method of access to the information. The main body of a dictionary is arranged alphabetically. With this arrangement and the type of information provided, a dictionary does not need to have an index. The table of contents, lists of figures and tables, and a unified or multiple indexes provide other points of access to the information in the resource. A unified index in a book includes all of the references to the text. Multiple indexes could separate the information into places, people, and subjects. All of these elements provide points of access to the information and should be logical and easily usable for you and your students.

How many of these print concepts carry over to an electronic reference source? What additional features and access points does the electronic resource add? How does searching work in the electronic resource? Entering a search term and getting a result should be easy to do. What steps are involved in modifying the search? Is there faceted searching to narrow the results? Is it easy to use, understand, and undo? Results lists can be long and intimidating to work with. Can the results list be sorted in a number of different orders so students can choose what works best for them? Can results be printed, e-mailed, saved, or exported. Are these options easy to find and use?

The arrangement of information is clearly an important decision and one that requires a lot of thought before the creation of the resource and a lot of work while creating the resource. In any format, the arrangement of information in an individual article and the arrangement of information in the whole reference resource should help you find and understand that information. All the pieces should support each other to make the whole a better work.

Cost

Cost is the final evaluation element. Cost is the initial up-front charge for the resource, any ongoing charges associated with the resource, and the anticipated value of the resource. Cost can easily influence a purchase decision.

If presented with the choice of two good resources on sports history, would you buy the $500 one or the $200 one that will leave you with an additional $300 to spend on other resources?

Print resources have an initial flat cost. Each year you own a print resource, its costs go down compared to many electronic resources. Buying the Oxford English Dictionary (OED) in print will cost you $1,300. Buying the electronic version of the OED may cost $1,000 per year. In five years' time, your print OED still cost $1,300, but your electronic access to the OED has cost you $5,000. Worse yet, if you need cancel your electronic OED, you have nothing to show for it. If you choose to never buy a print OED again, you will have the print for as long as you care to keep it.

Electronic resources may be purchased, rented, or leased, with a rental being short-term access and a lease lasting for at least one year. You need to be aware of what kind of agreement you are signing when paying for a reference resource. You need to understand what each means. Often times, when you purchase an electronic resource, it may be yours in perpetuity just like a print resource, but there is a hosting fee. This is a fee charged by the publisher or service providers to maintain access to your resource on their servers. The fee can be built into the price of the item for five years or be based on the number of items you purchased. For example, if you have 6–10 items with a publisher, or service provider, they may charge you $100 per year to host those resources. It is important to remember to include the hosting fee in your calculations of the cost of an item.

Value is easy to calculate after the fact when it does you the least amount of good. Cost per use is an easy measure of value. Here is how to calculate cost per use. In this first example, your library has a print resource that cost $500 to purchase; you have had the resource for five years, and each year that you have owned it, it has been used 20 times. The purchase price of $500 divided by the total number of uses over the period of ownership, which is 20 uses a year for five years for a total of 100 uses, yields the cost per use. That is $500/100, or $5 cost per use for the lifetime of the item. If you keep that reference resource for another year and it receives another 20 uses, then the cost per use for its lifetime drops to $4.17.

We need to calculate cost per use per year for print resources, because that is directly comparable to the cost per use figures we will calculate on the resources that we pay for annually. In our book example, the cost per use for the lifetime of the item was $5 per use. If we divide that number by the number of years we have owned the item, in this case, five years, then the cost per use per year is $1. The final equation should look like this: Cost/Years owned/Total uses. Total uses may be expressed as Years owned × Uses per year. The equation would now look like this: Cost/Years owned/(Years owned × Uses per year).

To calculate the cost per use of an electronic resource with an annual lease cost of $5,000, divide the cost by the number of uses. If your electronic resource is a database that receives 10,000 uses a year, then your cost per use per year is $5,000/10,000, or $.50 per use per year. If the electronic resource is an e-book with a flat cost of $200 and a hosting fee, the calculation is a little more difficult. Take the total of the cost plus the percentage of the annual hosting fee that represents one e-book. If you have 10 e-books and the hosting fee is $200 per year, then the hosting fee for each e-book is $200/10, or $20. Next divide $200 + $20 by the uses per year, or for the purposes of this example 4. Thus, our cost per use is $220/4, or $55 per use per year. For multiple years of ownership of an e-book with a hosting fee, the equation is (Cost + [Percent of hosting fee per item × Years owned])/Years owned/(Years owned × Uses per year). If we owned this $200 e-book for five years and it continues to get four uses per year, then the cost per use per year is ($200 + [$20 × 5])/5/(5 × 4), or $300/5/20, which is $3 cost per use per year.

Cost per use is a great way to determine the value you have received from an item. The lower the cost per use, the better the value you have received. If an item has a high cost per use, then it can be a candidate for weeding. There is not set cost per use that is too high. You determine what is too much for you to pay. There are few reasons to get rid of an item you own because of its cost per use, unless it is a print resource, and you need the shelf space. If it is a lease, then consider it for cancelation.

You can create a cost per use scenario for anticipated use based on your knowledge of the usage similar resources have received. In this case, you are projecting an anticipated value based on how much use you think the resource will receive. This can be a good method to help you make a purchase decision. Keep in mind that the bigger and more general a resource is, the bigger its appeal may be. A general database should appeal to more users than a specific e-book source does. A general print encyclopedia should garner more interest than a specific subject handbook.

EXAMPLES

There are many factors to consider when evaluating information or an information resource for quality. The five elements of evaluation work together to give you and your students a comprehensive picture of the quality of the information or resource. Evaluation is a difficult skill to master. The more you evaluate resources, the easier it becomes to apply the evaluation guidelines and judge the quality of the information or resource. This skill is one that you need to master and one that you should be helping your students to learn. Evaluation is fundamental to information literacy.

A checklist is a simple tool to help you evaluate information and resources. If a current, peer-reviewed article has a credentialed author and an extensive up-to-date bibliography, then you can put a check mark by Validity. However, some authors feel that checklists make the process too easy and lead to surface evaluations. For example, Meola (2004) states that using the checklist model "can serve to promote a mechanical and algorithmic way of evaluation that is at odds with the higher-level judgment and intuition that we presumably seek to cultivate as part of critical thinking." Burkholder (2010) points out that checklists reduce identification of quality sources to a "rigid" prototypical model. If the information in the source does not follow this formula, then it is of questionable quality.

A checklist can lead to rote thinking about evaluation, and some parts of the evaluation process are rote in nature. Deep thinking is generally not needed when it comes to currency, as an example. Because part of the checklist is quantitative, be sure that you add a qualitative evaluation to your checklist to encourage deep thinking. For example, you can add a check box for a grade which indicates the overall quality assessment of the information and then include a space where students justify the grade they gave to the article. Why does the information deserve an "A"? Why is it better than other information they found? Example checklists for you and your students are given in Figures 8.1 and 8.2. Additionally, you can have students discuss the grade they give to a resource in small groups. The process of discussion should encourage deeper thinking.

The following examples should help you apply the elements of evaluation. A high school student is doing a paper on capital punishment; the student finds a Web site he or she likes but is not sure whether it is good enough for his or her paper. The student asks for your help, and you look at his or her site and notice three things right away. It is a .com, has no author, and no publication date. Do you have enough information to make a decision about the possible quality of this site? Would it make a difference if the site had an author, a publication date, or both? What if the site were a .edu or a .org? How would that affect your decision? What if it was a .gov?

Next, you are doing research for an important presentation you have to make to the school district on the value of school libraries. You find an article in a database that looks perfect, but when you click on the author's name, you find that this is the only article in the database that this author has written. Is that reason enough not to use it? What factors would this article have to include to make you want to use it? Would a bibliography be enough, or would it need to be an extensive quality bibliography? Would it need to be published in a respected journal as well? This is why we must learn to evaluate.

EVALUATION CHECKLIST

Use the checklists in Figures 8.1 and 8.2 to help you and your students evaluate information resources. If you think a resource meets the standard for quality for that guideline, put a check mark in the box; otherwise, leave it blank.

Figure 8.1. Evaluation Checklist for Students

Item being evaluated:

Relevance	☐ Relevant	Does this item help me with my research? Why or why not?
Purpose	☐ Type of resource ☐ Style ☐ Scope	What type of resource is this, and how much of my topic is covered?
Validity	☐ Timeliness ☐ Accuracy ☐ Authority	Is the information up to date and accurate? Who wrote it and published it? What are his or her qualifications?
Grade	☐ A ☐ B ☐ C ☐ D ☐ F	What is the overall quality of the item, and what evidence supports this judgment?

Figure 8.2. Evaluation Checklist for Librarians

Resource being evaluated:

Relevance	☐ Relevant	Who is going to use this resource and for what types of research?
Purpose	☐ Type of resource ☐ Style ☐ Scope	What is the intended purpose of the resource, and is that appropriate for the library?
Validity	☐ Timeliness ☐ Accuracy ☐ Authority	Is the information accurate and up to date? What is the pedigree of the author and publisher?
Usability	☐ Format ☐ Arrangement	Is the resource easy to use and logically arranged?
Cost	☐ Initial cost ☐ Ongoing cost ☐ Value	What is the total cost of this resource, and does that represent a good value?
Grade	☐ A ☐ B ☐ C ☐ D ☐ F	What is the overall quality of the resource, and what evidence supports this judgment?

Write any notes that support your opinion about the information or resource, pro or con, in the third column. There are sample questions included in the third column to stimulate thinking about the evaluation element. However, your students may be better served if the questions are removed before using the checklist. Sample questions tend to end up reinforcing the checklist mentality of surface thinking and do not encourage students to think of multiple possibilities. When you have filled out the form, you should have a better picture of the quality and usefulness of the resource. The form in Figure 8.1 is for your students to use. The form in Figure 8.2 includes additional categories and is for you to use when evaluating resources for your library.

Vocabulary

accuracy

audience

authority

breadth

cost

depth

point of view

primary document

primary research

purpose

relevance

scope

secondary document

style

timeliness

tone of voice

type of resource

usability

validity

Questions

You have two items in your collection that you would like to update. Both of them are 10 years old. The first is a book about dinosaurs. The second is a book about U.S. history. You have enough money to update only one of the items. Which item would you update? How would timeliness effect your decision?

The World Almanac has an index, which is something you would expect to find in an almanac. However, the unique thing about the index in *The World Almanac* is that it is at the front of the book, or at least it was until the 2003 edition moved the index to the back of the volume. This illustrates the intellectual nature of arrangement. Someone decided that the book would be better with the index placed at the beginning, and then someone decided that it would be better with the index in its traditional location at the back. Do you understand why these choices were made? Which do you think is the better placement?

Which element of evaluation do you think is the most important and why?

What credentials are good enough for an author to have to give authority to an article on shark behavior?

How would you use cost per use to help you make a purchase decision?

Assignment

Pick a print resource and an electronic resource and then evaluate them thoroughly. Include cost, an anticipated cost per use, and your purchase decision.

Find a newspaper, news magazine, scholarly journal article, and two Web sites with different domains on the same topic. Use the Evaluation Checklist for Students and evaluate the information found in each source. Include a paragraph describing which information source you found to be the best and why.

Chapter 9

Finding Answers and Using Information Ethically

This chapter examines what an answer is, how to find and extract information from a source, and how to use that information ethically.

ANSWERING A QUESTION FROM THE LIBRARIAN'S POINT OF VIEW

As librarians, we know how to answer questions, and we know what answers are. If someone asks us what 2 + 2 is, we answer 4. If someone asks us what the meaning of life is, we quote Douglas Adams, answer 42, and then show the customer where the philosophy books are. Librarians are very focused on answers. It is our job to provide them, but what exactly constitutes an answer?

If a student asks a research question, what is our answer? Do we do the research for the student, or do we already have a stack of the best materials available on that topic ready to hand? Although these may be the best answers to the student's question, it is not the answer we provide. Our answer is to show the student how to use a database, get him or her started by helping find a few good articles, then suggesting that he or she keep going, and if he or she needs any more help, he or she should come back to the desk and ask another question.

An answer to a reference question for a librarian, then, is not necessarily the answer to the question being asked, but the provision of some information literacy instruction in a recommended resource and following up with the customer later. This is standard operating procedure. This is the correct answer to a question that does not have one answer and involves synthesizing information from multiple sources. However, is this the answer that our customers expect?

ANSWERING A QUESTION FROM THE STUDENT'S POINT OF VIEW

Questions should have concrete answers from the student's point of view. Being told to look in a particular resource and good luck is not an answer to his or her question. The research process is new, and the idea of having to read multiple sources to assemble his or her answer is difficult to understand. Why would students want to ask librarians questions if the answers they receive are so obtuse? Perhaps this is a reason why students may see librarians as unhelpful or providing incorrect answers.

To overcome this perception, we need to explain the research process to our customers as well as teach them research skills. Another approach is to help younger students find the answer within resources. For example, a young student asks what the 10 most popular breeds of dogs are and why. We can help the student find a concrete answer to the first part of the question. This gives us the opportunity to teach how to use the resource and locate information within a resource, which is an important research skill and part of the Big6 Skills.

Then we can provide the student with the resource that talks about the personalities and characteristics of each breed of dog. We can show the student how to find dog breeds within this resource, and how the information for each entry is arranged so that he or she can find information about the personality of each dog from the list of the top 10 breeds. We are not giving the student the answer in this case, but we have showed him or her how to find it and where to find it. We are leaving to the student to extract the information from the resource this time.

In this example, we have provided an answer and taught a student how to use resources, find information within resources, extract that information, and learn how to extract information for himself or herself. We have built a foundation that will help the student progress with information literacy skills as he or she moves through middle school and high school, and we ask the student to do more complex research tasks that do require abstract thought. The student should already have the skills necessary to know how to extract information and now is old enough to have developed abstract thinking abilities (Harper 2011). The student's new-found mental prowess combined with information literacy skills makes the process of extracting abstract information an extension of his or her improving information literacy skills.

It is not the job of the elementary school librarian to teach students everything they need to know about information literacy. Information literacy skills are a continuum. They should improve with students' mental abilities and with the increasing difficulty of information needs. However, learning to use information ethically does not require abstract thinking. It can and should be taught to young students to develop good habits that will last a lifetime.

THE ETHICAL USE OF INFORMATION

Teaching students how to use information ethically is part of our definition of information literacy. It is, therefore, an important and a necessary part of becoming information literate. The ethical use of information involves being aware of copyright and fair use and giving others credit when you use their ideas.

Copyright, Fair Use, and Terms of Use Agreements

Copyright is a form of intellectual property, which is "creations of the mind" (World Intellectual Property Organization 2011). Copyright is the legal protections granted to the creators of original works that include "literary, dramatic, musical, artistic and certain other intellectual works" (U.S. Copyright Office 2008). Under these rights, the copyright holder may allow other persons to display, perform, copy, or create derivative forms of the work by turning a novel into a movie, for example. Copyright is implied. It does not have to be applied for and granted. Any original creation that falls within the bounds of copyright is automatically granted the rights that come with copyright. Copyright starts the moment a work is "fixed in a copy," which is an "object from which a work can be read" (U.S. Copyright Office 2008).

Fair use is an important limitation of copyright that directly affects the work of school librarians. Fair use grants each person limited rights to use a copyrighted work. This includes using the work for the purpose of scholarship or research (U.S. Copyright Office 2009). Fair use has four factors that need to be considered to determine if the use of the work is not a copyright violation. The first is the nature of the use you plan to put the material to. Works used in schools and in class are not being used for commercial gain but for educational purposes. This supports fair use. The nature of the document is the second factor. Documents that are largely factual have less protection under fair use. Facts and ideas cannot be copyrighted. It is the expression of those ideas, the word choice, and the sentence structure that receive the copyright.

The third factor is the amount of the work to be used. The smaller the piece of the work you intend to use, the more fair use as a copyright exemption applies. Some librarians use guidelines like no more than 10 percent of the work can be used. However, guidelines are not part of the law. There is no correct amount that you are allowed to use. The fourth and final factor is how your use of the copyrighted work affects its market value. Copying an entire work and distributing it to a class does have an impact on that work's market value, but using a few chapters or some parts of the work may help promote sales. The four factors should be evaluated together to determine if the use you are planning for an item is fair. When weighing this information, if you think that the use is fair, then chances are that you are probably right. Your role as school librarians has also given you the role of school authority on copyright. You need to stay informed on copyright laws and fair use for the benefit of your school.

One of these areas you need to know about is terms of use agreements. These agreements can eliminate copyright protections. This is a good topic to present to a class as it covers an aspect of information literacy that may be unknown to students. When you or a student signs up for a social networking site, you have to agree to the terms of service before an account is created. The terms of service may say that whatever you post, whether it is in your account or a comment on a post from someone else's account, belongs to the service provider. The service provider owns your creative work and your unique and original expression and has the right to create derivative works from it. In other words, the service provider can create a book from the ideas posted by multiple users of the site and sell the book for a profit while not having to share any of those profits with the creators of the content. You and your students have signed away your copyright by agreeing to the terms of service. This is an important lesson in information literacy for the technological age we live in.

Works published before 1923 are in the public domain (Hirtle 2013). This means that the works are no longer protected by copyright and may be used in any manner. Another option that was spawned by our technological age allows authors to assign their works a Creative Commons license. If you go to the Web page created by Hirtle, you will see that he has used a Creative Commons Attribution license, which allows anyone to use the work for any purpose as long as he or she credits the original author's work (Creative Commons 2013). Government documents are not covered by copyright law. They are in the public domain. Whether an item is in the public domain, has a Creative Commons license, or is copyrighted, students need to use their sources ethically, and that means they need to quote their sources accurately and cite them correctly; otherwise, they have committed plagiarism.

Plagiarism

Plagiarism is not illegal. Your students will not go to jail if they are caught plagiarizing. Plagiarism is stealing and taking credit for the ideas or words of another as if they were your own (Merriam-Webster, Inc. 2013c). It is unethical, and the real-world consequences of plagiarism can be severe. A high-ranking official in the German government, Defense Minister Karl-Theodor zu Guttenberg, was forced to resign his cabinet position in March 2011, because he plagiarized information in his doctoral thesis (Dempsey 2011). Another German cabinet member had to resign her post in 2013 over plagiarism allegations. This time it was Annett Schavan, the minister for education and research (Jump and Symington 2013).

These examples may be too removed from your students' lives for them to be able to relate to the issue. Kaavya Viswanathan had her young adult novel published right after graduating from high school and before she became a student at Harvard University ("How Opal Mehta Got Kissed, Got Wild, and Got a Life" 2013). When it was discovered that passages were plagiarized, the book was recalled, and her publishing contract was canceled. She claimed that the plagiarism was unconscious (Glazer 2013). Punishments for plagiarism at the college level range from the mild to the moderate to the severe, from getting a zero on the assignment the student plagiarized to receiving a failing grade in that class to being dismissed from the university.

In his article, Minkel (2002) reported on a 2001 survey done by Rutgers University of 4,471 high school students that found "more than half had stolen sentences and paragraphs from the Internet." A paper published in *CQ Researcher* states that more than two-thirds of college students admit to cheating, or plagiarism, and that the number of college students who admit to cheating has dropped, because of the perception that plagiarism is not cheating. College students' most common justification for plagiarizing is that it was unintentional (Glazer 2013).

Why do students plagiarize? A fascinating article looked at this question from the perspective of rational choice theory and developed an equation which states that the probability of plagiarizing is equal to the utility that plagiarism offers, minus the norms against that behavior, plus the opportunities that students have to plagiarize (Sattler, Graeff, and Willen 2013). Utility is the perceived benefit that would be derived from plagiarizing versus the chance of getting caught. Opportunity is the number of chances the students have to plagiarize. Finally, norms are the social and cultural standards against cheating. The researchers found that an increase of one standard deviation to utility increases the likelihood of plagiarism by 96 percent, while a similar increase to the norm decreases the likelihood of plagiarism only by 45 percent.

This research indicates that librarians and teachers need to make plagiarism harder to get away with and increase the prohibition against it. There are services like Turnitin (http://turnitin.com) that compare student papers to papers of others in the class, and others in their database of student papers, the Web, and scholarly databases to find plagiarized passages and sentences (iParadigms 2013). Warning students that assignments will be checked using Turnitin should help discourage plagiarism. Teaching students what plagiarism is and what the consequences of plagiarizing are should raise the norm against this form of cheating. Teaching students that plagiarism is easy to avoid by citing sources should also decrease this behavior.

CITING SOURCES

Citing the source of a quote or an idea gives that author the credit he or she deserves for the idea, and it avoids plagiarism. A citation is a bibliographic reference to the work where the quote or idea came from. Citations have two parts, an in-text portion and a bibliography. The in-text citation is very brief. It includes the author's name and the year of publication, or it may be as simple as a number. The name or number is then used to find the full reference to the resource in an alphabetically arranged bibliography or in a numerically arranged end notes. The full bibliographic information includes the author's name, the title of the work, the name of the publication, date of the publication, and other information depending on the source and the citation style used.

There are thousands of citation styles. Each one has its specific set of rules for what information to record, how to record it, how the in-text citation looks, and how the bibliography is organized. Some of the styles cover an entire disciple, whereas others are used only by a single journal title. The American Psychological Association (APA) developed a style for psychology, the APA style, and it is used in many of the other social sciences. The Modern Language Association (MLA) created a style used in English classes and often encountered by students because of the writing requirements of English classes. The concept of citing sources is much easier to understand than the intricacies and extreme pickiness of actually creating a citation.

Citation Resources

Librarians need to know all about citations, citation resources, and the reason for citing in the first place, because we will be answering questions about how to cite, showing students where to find help with their cites, and teaching them why they need to cite in the first place as part of our information literacy instruction to them. Fortunately, there are many resources to help students with citations. First, there are books from the style creators that explain every detail of the style and how to cite many different kinds of resources in their format. There is the *MLA Handbook* for the style created by the Modern Language Association and the *Publication Manual* written by the APA for its style. These books are the ultimate authority and therefore may be too detailed and beyond the needs of the average student. There are books like *A Pocket Style Manual* that covers APA, MLA, and Chicago styles without all the depth of association-produced resources, but with more than enough detail for students to get the styles correct.

Web sites like *Research and Documentation Online* (http://bcs.bedfordstmartins.com/resdoc5e) provide detailed help with the major formats by providing easy-to-find examples to answer any citation-related questions. Other Web sites provide citation style guides, one- or two-page guides to a style with examples covering basic formats. Purdue University's Online Writing Lab, known as OWL (http://owl.english.purdue.edu/owl/), has provided guides to APA and MLA for years and is referenced by many other Web sites.

Commercial databases, like EBSCOhost's *Academic Search Premier*, generate a bibliographic citation for an individual resource or a list of resources in the major styles. This last option could generate the entire bibliography for a research paper if the student used sources only from this database. Students will love this feature, but they need to be warned that not all the citations generated by these databases are accurate. They still need to be taught the basics of the style so that they can spot the errors in the citations generated by the database.

There are Web resources, citation generators, that create citations one at a time but with great accuracy. Usually, students need to input the citation information for the item to receive the properly formatted citation. Students can save the individual citation and add others to it to build a bibliography. These resources also show the in-text cite, and both the in-text cite and the bibliography can be copied into a student's paper. Resources like Son of Citation Machine (http://citationmachine.net), Noodle Tools (http://www.noodletools.com), and EasyBib (http://www.easybib.com) have shortcuts for finding books and other materials to make the process easier. Some of these services are free, and others charge a fee for upgraded services that support all of your students with individual accounts.

Zotero (https://www.zotero.org/) is a freeware program that helps students not only generate in-text cites and bibliographies but also track their research. It is too much for elementary and middle school students but should work well in high school and beyond. Zotero is in a class of software known as citation managers or citation management software. There are commercial programs in this category, EndNote (http://endnote.com) and RefWorks (http://www.refworks.com), that support thousands of styles (Thomson Reuters 2013). These programs include features called cite-while-you-write that insert in-text citations into your word-processing document as you write and then generate the bibliography from those in-text sources. This is a valuable and time-saving feature. In addition, these programs will import citation information from commercial databases and, in the case of Zotero, from Web sites. Most of these programs are designed for college students and research professionals.

All of these resources are subject to the axiom "garbage in, garbage out" to some degree. When you import an article that has its title in all capital letters in the database into one of these programs, the citation generated by the citation manager may keep the all-capital-letter format, which is incorrect in every style. Again, this is why it is so important to know what a proper citation should look like and to have multiple resources available to consult.

Quoting, Paraphrasing, and Summarizing

Extracting information from a resource is one of the information literacy skills that school librarians need to teach their students. It is clearly tied to citing sources. Students pull the information from the resources, use it in their project to answer their information need, and then cite the source of the information. Teaching students how to properly include, and cite the information they want to use in their project, is showing them the correct way to extract information from a resource.

Students can show the information they extracted and used in their paper in three ways: a quote, a paraphrase, or a summary of the information from the source. A quote should be an exact word for word copy of a phrase, sentence, or even a paragraph from the information source. Copy and paste is a skill that students develop early, but they must remember to enclose this direct copy within double quotation marks. A quote lends authority to the argument and is important to use when the exact wording from an article makes the student's point. Quoting is the easiest skill for students to use.

Paraphrasing is more difficult than quoting. A paraphrase is a restatement of the author's meaning in the student's own words. A student may want to consider paraphrasing when the author's statement is long, and can be shortened, or needs to be shortened for the sake of clarity or brevity. It is important that a paraphrase is in the student's own words. The student should not use the phrasing the author used in the passage he or she wishes to paraphrase. If the student cannot think of another way to express the point, then he or she should be taught to use a quote.

Summarizing the information found in a source is the final option students have for extracting information. A summary is an abstract of the information source. It is a short description written in the students own words, not a copy of the abstract, that summarizes the main points or findings of the source. A summary represents the entire information source or, at its smallest, a chapter within a source. A paraphrase, on the other hand, represents a passage or single idea within the information source. That is what distinguishes one from the other. Summaries require students to have critical thinking skills. They need to understand the point the author is making and be able to boil it down into a few sentences. Summarizing is the hardest of the three extracting skills. A student may want to summarize an information source when all he or she wants to present is the findings of that source. A literature review, a standard part of many research papers, summarizes the findings of many information sources to support the hypotheses of the paper.

The ethical use of information is an important part of information literacy. It is also broad, ranging from copyright law to quoting a source. The concepts involved in the ethical use of information also range from easy to difficult and fussy to demanding. It is a multileveled and multifaceted skill that needs to be introduced in stages, practiced, and reinforced throughout a student's education.

Vocabulary

bibliography

citation generators

citation managers

citation styles

citing

copyright

ethical use of information

extracting information

fair use

intellectual property

in-text citation

paraphrase

plagiarism

public domain

quote

summarize

terms of use

Questions

What constitutes unethical information behavior?

Has technology changed students' views of plagiarism? If so, why?

What do you think the consequences of plagiarism should be for students in high school? Should it be the same for middle school students?

When should you introduce students to summarizing, and when do you think they should be able to do it well?

Assignment

Find an information source and then use any four methods to automatically generate a citation, for example, the database's citation generator, Son of Citation Machine, EasyBib, and Zotero. Compare all four citations. Are they all the same? Are they all correct? Which one was the easiest to use? Which one generated the best citation? Which one would you recommend to your students?

Write a lesson plan for teaching sixth grader about the ethical use of information. Then write a lesson plan on the same topic for high school juniors. Each lesson plan should include an activity for the students that supports the lesson.

Chapter 10

Information Literacy Instruction

This chapter provides an overview of library instruction, how it is an extension of your reference services, and why it is an important part of what school librarians should do. Learning theory, types of instruction, and lesson planning are also examined.

WHAT IS INFORMATION LITERACY INSTRUCTION?

Information literacy (IL) instruction is a planned instruction session for multiple recipients in a formal setting with the goal of imparting IL skills. If we define reference service in the same terminology, then the definition would be as follows: reference service is the spontaneous instruction of one or more recipients in an informal setting with the goal of imparting IL skills while answering a specific question. One of the differences between IL instruction and reference services is in the numbers. Reference is a one-to-one relationship. IL instruction, on the other hand, is a one-to-many relationship. This relationship is potentially an efficient method to impart IL skills, more efficient than reference service.

This is an important reason to engage in IL instruction. It gives you the chance to provide reference service to a group of students all at the same time. However, it is done before the question has been asked, making it a form of preemptive reference. IL instruction seeks to provide students the reference help they would receive when they ask a question, but it does so in anticipation of the question that will be asked. This is a problem with IL instruction. What if you answer the wrong question or your instruction takes place a month before the students need the information?

Planned versus spontaneous is the other differences between the IL instruction and the reference service. Planning for IL instruction gives you a chance to prepare a lesson plan to reach your curricular goals, to help the teacher of the class to reach his or her curricular goals, and, most important, to help students with their projects. It gives you a chance to work with the teacher to plan for when the instruction will occur, what project the students will be working on, what information resources will be covered, and how you will engage with the students on their project.

Although IL instruction can be thought of as preemptive reference, that is not the point. It should not lower the number of questions you receive at the reference desk. In fact, good IL instruction should encourage students to ask more questions and should increase the number of questions you receive at the reference desk. The questions you receive should be different in nature. Library instruction should help "raise the level of complexity of the questions that remain" (Grassian and Kaplowitz 2001).

A VERY BRIEF HISTORY OF INFORMATION LITERACY INSTRUCTION

IL instruction has been called bibliographic instruction, and it was called library instruction before it became information literacy instruction. The terminology helps us to understand the history of the concept. Bibliographies were of primary importance in finding library resources many years ago. You consulted a bibliography to find books. Around the turn of the nineteenth century, we began to see indexes to the periodical literature. As this type of bibliography grew in number, importance, and size through the twentieth century, we began to think of bibliographic instruction as old fashioned. We needed a new term and used library instruction to represent the broader resources available to our customers. This change in name reflected a change in resources but not the nature of research. The term "information literacy" came into use in the 1980s. Not only had the resources changed in nature with the growth of databases, but the concept of the value of library skills also changed. IL instruction is a name that reflects this broader conception of information skills and their importance to other disciplines and society.

IL instruction, like reference service, has been around for a long time. There are reports of library instruction in German universities as far back as the seventeenth century (Lorenzen 2001). In the United States, Harvard was doing library instruction in the 1820s (Salony 1995). This was the era of bibliographic instruction, and it lasted a very long time.

Melvil Dewey, among his many accomplishments, was the first to express in 1876 that the "library is a school, and the librarian is in the highest sense a teacher" (Grassian and Kaplowitz 2001). In 1912, William Bishop, the Librarian of Congress, worried about the exponential growth of materials which he called the "literary deluge" and the need for library instruction (Grassian and Kaplowitz 2001). In 1939, Carter Alexander concerned about equipping our elementary school students to deal with "modern life" saw the need for projects that "require the use of a great many library materials" and not just the prescribed textbook (1939). Alexander went on to say that "Training elementary-school children to use library materials effectively is a co-operative job, its success depending on the team work of various persons. These individuals are the pupil, his teachers, his principal, his superintendent, his school librarian, other librarians involved, and his parents" (1939). Even though these ideas are more than 70 years old, they mirror our current thinking about our roles and the purpose of IL instruction.

LEARNING THEORIES

To provide quality library instruction, it is important to have background knowledge of learning theory and teaching. For many school librarians, this is the easy part. You already have teaching experience, degrees, and certificates. Academic librarians and public librarians need not have this background, and teaching may be new to them and to some of you. In fact, library school students may not receive any instruction in teaching. Julien (2005) found that about 52 percent of library schools do *not* offer a course in IL instruction. In the schools that do offer a course in IL instruction, only one school required the course as part of the degree program. In the passing years since this article was published, it is hoped that this situation has changed. In any event, there is a need for librarians to have an understanding of teaching.

Behaviorism

The first of the four learning theories we will examine is behaviorism. Behaviorism is the oldest of the four theories. In the behaviorist model, learning happens "when prompted by a stimulus and shaped by repetition/reinforcement" (Giustini 2008). Rewards are given to reinforce desirable behaviors. Rewards can be praise or good grades. Behaviorism is also associated with punishment for not doing the desired behavior.

Behaviorism is a passive learning model (Eryaman and Genc 2013). Teaching is done to students, and they should respond with the correct answer. Behaviorists believe that "behavior can be studied in a systematic and observable way without considering internal mental states or cognitive processes of the learner" (Eryaman and Genc 2013). Another resource states that behaviorism is active. It is about doing. It is learning via trial and error and interaction (Kaplowitz 2008). Both are right if you look at the process. Behaviorism is active. It is about doing the selected process. It is passive, in that students respond to a stimulus that is put upon them by their teachers.

Behaviorism is associated with the traditional lecture method of teaching. Famous behaviorists are Ivan Pavlov, John B. Watson, and B. F. Skinner. Behaviorism works well for computer-aided instruction because it allows for repetition, and positive reinforcement can be built in (Giustini 2008).

Cognitivism

Cognitivism was a response to behaviorism. Learning in cognitivist theory is "an internal mental organization of knowledge, stressing the acquisition of knowledge, mental structures, and processing of information" (Eryaman and

Genc 2013). Learning is an active, though internal, process built upon prior knowledge, experience, and observation of the situation to answer questions or solve puzzles. It is about insight and having an "aha" moment (Kaplowitz 2008).

Jean Piaget is a famous cognitivist. He believed that students' minds developed in stages, and these different mental stages correspond with a growth from concrete thinking to abstract thinking. Cognitivism is a student-centered learning model.

Constructivism

Constructivism is a form of cognitivism. It is also student centered, but it rejects the Piaget theory of learning stages. Contructivists believe that learners construct meaning and test their understanding in social situations. Learning is dependent upon having the right opportunities and experience to learn, and not on developmental stages (Kaplowitz 2008). Learners are "active creators of their own knowledge" (Eryaman and Genc 2013). Constructivism embraces the social and cultural nature of learning and takes the context of learning and information into consideration.

Lev Vygotsky and John Dewey (no relation to Melvil) are two famous constructivists. Dewey believed that teachers should help students "think for themselves." He focused on experiential learning and reflection on the experience to deepen the learning (Giustini 2008).

Humanism

Humanism recognizes that feeling and emotional states affect learning. Humanism takes a holistic approach to student learning addressing the intellect, emotions, social life, artistic, and practical skills of the students to create learning, and develop self-esteem ("Humanistic Education" 2013). Abraham Maslow is a famous humanist. His hierarchy of needs is an important psychological concept. In terms of education, if the lower needs are not met, needs like food, shelter, and safety, then higher needs like self-esteem and self-actualization cannot be met (Kaplowitz 2008).

Maslow identified the qualities of a good teacher as empathy, care for the student, and genuineness ("Humanistic Education" 2013). Genuineness also translates to having authentic learning activities. Students in the humanistic classroom should not only have a student-centered learning environment but also have self-directed learning opportunities. Humanism is about self, motivation, and goals ("Humanism" 2013).

All four of these learning theories coexist. Though their creators hoped to replace existing theories with their own, they failed in this endeavor. This is a good indication that no one theory is completely correct. Each theory has its strengths and weaknesses. Examining these four learning theories shows that they have commonalities. Active learning is one of the concepts they all embrace. Clearly, it is an important concept to use in your teaching. Beyond that, pick and choose the most important ideas and concepts from each of the theories to build your own learning theory that addresses all aspects of learning.

LEARNING STYLES

Learning styles are the ways that students acquire, process, and retain information. The assumption is that all learners have a preferred learning style, a method of acquiring information that works best for them. Cognitive styles is another term that is frequently used for learning styles, but cognitive styles refer only to processing and organizing information; therefore, it is a subset of learning styles (Hollins 2012).

There are many learning styles. David Kolb classified learners into four categories, divergers, assimilators, convergers, and accommodators (Small et al. 2012). Anthony Gregorc's model proposes two perceptual qualities, concrete and abstract, and two ordering abilities, random and sequential ("Learning Styles" 2013). The two perceptual qualities are combined with the two ordering abilities to create four categories of learners, for example, a concrete sequential or an abstract random. There are right brain and left brain styles, with right brain learners being holistic and pattern oriented and left brain learners being analytical and detail oriented (Kaplowitz 2008).

Perhaps the most well-known learning style is Neil Fleming's VAK model. This model proposes that there are three types of learners, visual learners, auditory learners, and kinesthetic learners. Fleming believed that visual learners think in pictures and want to see information. Auditory learners learn best by listening to information being presented. Kinesthetic learners need to do, to touch in order to learn ("Learning Styles" 2013).

Kaplowitz categorizes the learning styles into three broad categories, physiological, cognitive, and affective, which correspond to how learners interact, think, and feel about their world and also correspond to the learning theories of the behaviorists, constructivists, and humanists (Kaplowitz 2008). This approach helps one to understand both learning theories and learning styles.

However, there is a problem with learning styles. Most librarians believe in the validity of learning styles at a rate of about 71 percent (Dalrymple 2002). The problem is that learning styles have not been shown to be valid. The instruments that determine a person's preferred learning style are not trustworthy (Hollins 2012). As for the learning styles themselves, a panel convened to evaluate learning styles found that most research on the topic did not use a valid research design, and of the few that did, only one was a positive finding, supporting learning styles. All the others were negative findings, indicating that the theories of learning styles are not valid ("Learning Styles" 2013). The idea that some people learn better visually and some better auditorily "has not been strongly supported experimentally" (MacLeod 2004). Susan Greenfield, a neuroscientist, called learning styles "nonsense" and said that "humans have evolved to build a picture of the world through our senses working in unison, exploiting the immense interconnectivity that exists in the brain" ("Learning Styles" 2013). Finally, research has shown little benefit for students (Hollins 2012) and no significant learning differences between congruent and incongruent groups of students ("Learning Styles" 2013).

What does this mean for our teaching? If you were a visual learner who loved to see charts and graphs, because you really "see" the information in them, how would you react to an hour-long presentation that was nothing but charts and graphs? Would you get bored or enjoy it? Would you lose focus and miss half of the information presented, or would you retain it all? Would you prefer that the presenter break up the presentation of charts and graphs with some lectures or a video? Research has shown that students retain only 5 percent of the material learned in a lecture (Small et al. 2012), but how much would you retain from an all-audio presentation? We can learn in any environment with any instructional method. To keep students interested and engaged in the lesson, vary the teaching method. Since we learn through all of our senses, engage them all. This is the lesson of learning styles.

LEARNING ENVIRONMENTS

The traditional learning environment is the classroom where we give students face-to-face instruction. The new learning environments were all the result of technological change. Since they are technology based, some have come and gone, like two-way video connection. It has been replaced with better, more efficient technology.

Face-to-face instruction has been around as long as there has been teaching. It is still the preferred learning environment. It allows students to interact with each other and their teachers. It allows for immediate feedback. Teachers can see if the students have understood what they said, and if not, offer another example. It is the most flexible learning environment because many different teaching methods can be employed.

Online learning has developed rapidly in the past few years. Learning management systems (LMSs) have been developed to make creating a course or a lesson easy for the teacher while supporting many student-centered functions. An LMS can be accessed from anywhere in the world at any time. Material can be reviewed as much as the student wants. Tests can grade themselves and provide immediate feedback. Other resources, like Turnitin, can be incorporated into the class, and group projects with peer grading can be assigned. LMSs offer many unique and useful features for instruction, but they also assume a minimum level of technology, access, and knowledge.

A blended environment uses face-to-face instruction supplemented by an LMS. This method allows teachers to use the best of both worlds. They can offer an engaging and a diverse face-to-face experience with lesson plans, supporting materials, and instant feedback quizzes in the LMS.

The flipped classroom is currently a very popular approach to instruction that changes up the learning environment. In the flipped classroom, students watch a video of the lecture at home or during their free time. Then they spend class time working on the problems and getting help from the instruction. Flipped instruction is not new. Students have been given a reading, a lecture substitute, to prepare for a discussion in class the next day. Math classes often consist of a lecture and demonstration followed by class time to do the "homework." The flipped classroom has been given a boost by technology. It is easy to record a lecture or demonstration and post it online or in an LMS for students to view as long as they have access to the appropriate technology for viewing it.

INSTRUCTIONAL METHODS

In their book *Teaching for Inquiry*, Small et al. (2012) identify seven instructional methods. They are questioning, practice, discussion, brainstorming, role-playing, gaming, and lecture. Any of these methods may be combined with any number of the others. For example, a typical "lecture" may really consist of lecture, questioning, and discussion. A typical IL instruction session may consist of lecture, questioning, demonstration, and practice, which is hands-on time for doing. Demonstration is not one of the methods that Small et al. list, but we will include it.

Using questions to engage the class is the Socratic method. It is an effective way to get the class involved and to engage them in deeper thinking. Make eye contact when asking questions. Look from student to student, and wait for an answer. Give students a chance to reflect. Small et al. (2012) summarize the research done by Mary Budd Rowe, which found that teachers wait on average 0.9 seconds for students to answer a question. This encourages students to either not respond or blurt out any answer to meet their teachers' expectations of a quick answer. When responding to questions, provide meaningful feedback. Say more than "no," or "close," Say something more like "That's not correct, I think you need to consider this aspect" or "You're on the right track, but I need more information." This will guide student thinking and encourage more reflection.

Holding a classroom discussion or a brainstorming session on a topic is a good way to activate background knowledge and generate ideas about a topic. Interest should also be generated by these methods as students discover what they want to know. Your job is to facilitate in either case. Keep the students on track. All ideas should get to be expressed before the winnowing down and narrowing of focus begins.

Demonstration and practice go hand in hand and are valuable instructional tools. A demonstration shows students how a resource works. It models good, effective behavior and proper use of the resource, which includes the features you think will be of most value to your students. After the demonstration comes practice. This hands-on time gives students the chance to do and engage with the resource in a personal manner. It will reinforce the demonstration and also give students a chance to play, experiment, and succeed.

INSTRUCTIONAL STYLE

Instructional style is who you are when you teach. This is how you present yourself to your students. It is important that you be authentic, true to who you are, but there are some techniques that you need to remember and use. Just like with the reference transaction, you need to make eye contact with your students. Shift your focus from one to another. Give a student who is asking a question or answering a question your full attention. This shows the whole class that you respect and want their input. Smile whether you feel like it or not. Smiles help put your students at ease, help you feel better, and establish a connection with your students. You may be nervous, but remember that you are the expert. There is no reason that you should not project confidence in your knowledge, skills, and ability.

Carla List-Handley (2008) discusses teaching as performance. You are the actor presenting the play, and your stage is the classroom or instruction space. This perspective offers many good techniques for your instructional style. Instructor is a role you are playing. It is easier to project confidence when you accept that you are acting. The role you play can mask your nervousness. Like a good stage actor, you need to project your voice and speak clearly so your audience, your students, can hear and understand you. You should move about the stage and use gestures, but not to the point of distraction. If you speak with your hands, you need to curb that behavior and use gestures to highlight an important fact or to direct students' attention. Pacing is distracting, but moving purposely and in moderation about the classroom will help draw students' focus. Remember to stop and give your full attention when a student is speaking. If something does not go as planned, be ready and willing to improvise.

TYPES OF INFORMATION LITERACY INSTRUCTION

There are two types of IL instruction that we will address. The first is the single instruction session, and the second is a course of instruction. The single session is often called a one-shot instruction session, because you have only one shot at the students and one chance to present IL to those students. It is also called the one shot, because the classroom teacher does not want to give up any more class time than that. One hour is the typical time frame for the one shot. This does not allow for much time to cover important IL concepts and resources that will help students with their assignment. A general rule of thumb is not to present more than two concepts to the students and not to overwhelm them with the number of resources, but introduce them to a select number depending on what their project is.

It is important that the IL instruction take place when the students have a project or an assignment to complete. If you do general instruction on library resources at the beginning of the term, then chances are very good that students will not remember the information you covered when they start to work on their assignments a month or more later. Also, the likelihood that you covered resources they will actually need beyond an encyclopedia is slim. Reference is performed at the teachable moment. IL instruction needs to create the teachable moment and take advantage of it. The one-shot session can be expanded with asynchronous instruction, which we will discuss in Chapter 11.

A course of IL instruction is defined as any planned IL instruction that spans more than one session. Though this definition means that two sessions are a course, two sessions enable you to do twice as much and meet more instructional goals. A number of colleges offer credit-bearing courses in IL skills. This is an ideal method for meeting your IL curricular goals and to prepare students to meet the research requirements of their future courses. However, these classes are often taught in the absence of authentic research needs. As with the one shot, the information may be provided at an inopportune time and in too general fashion to be helpful when students need to use these skills.

A course of IL instruction has the benefit of time and allows you more opportunity to interact with students, to see what they have learned, how they are
progressing, and what you need to do to help them now. It gives you the chance
to examine progress toward meeting the goals of your lesson plans, and time to
make adjustments to them. Obviously meeting with a class three or more times
requires a much more substantial commitment of time, and time is a precious
commodity in schools.

THE BENEFITS OF INFORMATION LITERACY INSTRUCTION

This chapter has addressed many issues with IL instruction. This book has
talked about how important IL skills are for students, for creating lifelong learners and for developing active and informed participants in our democratic society. What has not been addressed is whether IL instruction actually improves
students' skills and achievement. Nor have we addressed why librarians should
teach IL skills.

There are many research articles that show student improvement after IL
instruction. We will look at a few. Here is a good example; this first study found
that college students who received IL instruction cited more sources, more
types of sources, and more books than their counterparts who did not receive
instruction, and they continue to cite more sources throughout their academic
career (Cooke and Rosenthal 2011). Another study with college students used
four groups of students: the control group that received no IL instruction, a
teacher instructed one-shot group, a librarian instructed one-shot group, and
finally, a group that took a course in library instruction on the Web (Mery,
Newby, and Peng 2012). As expected, the control group members showed no
improvement in their IL skills. Interestingly, neither did the group taught by
their course instructor instead of a librarian. The one-shot session led by a
librarian showed more than a 9 percent improvement in their skills, and the
students who took a course in IL showed a gain of about 23 percent.

The study by Mery, Newby, and Peng illustrates a number of interesting
points. First librarians need to conduct IL instruction. Teachers are content
experts in their field, and we are content experts in ours. Our field is IL, and
we should teach IL to others. We do it best. Next, we see that IL improves even
in a one-shot environment. Finally, the more chances we have to instruct students, the greater the improvement to their skills. There is another study that
shows that if students receive at least three or four library instruction session,
there is a strong possibility that were will be an improvement in their grade
point average (Wong and Cmor 2011).

Finally, a study of 6th through 12th graders participating in a guide inquiry
project at the libraries of 10 different schools in New Jersey found that the students had learned from the unit and, importantly, knew that they had learned.
Though what many of the students learned was an accumulation of facts, some
students did show a synthesis of the facts (Todd 2006). IL instruction works. It
improves students' IL skills, their homework, their knowledge of the topic, and
their grades. However, IL instruction is probably best performed as part of an
organized program.

A PROGRAM OF INFORMATION LITERACY INSTRUCTION

The difference between an IL instruction and an IL instruction program is scope. An IL instruction program should ensure that all of your students receive the necessary and important instruction they need and enable you to meet your curricular goals. The American Association of School Librarians (AASL) standards and their counterparts in the Common Core State Standards or your own state standards are your purview. In an IL program, you can plan what skills will be taught to which grades and find classes you can work with to impart those skills. An effective program in library instruction cannot be done in isolation. You need the support of administration and the cooperation of teachers in your school to take you from a simple one-shot lecture to a successful IL program.

If there is no IL instruction program at your school, start slow. Work with one or two teachers at first. Build your reputation for cooperation, and let teachers see the results your IL instruction sessions have on students' work and learning. Then reach out to other teachers, and grow your program. Take the results of your work to the administration, show them what you have achieved, and show them your roadmap to implementing a full program. Explain why it is a great idea for the school to have an IL program. Then all you need to do is continue doing great work.

Implementing an IL program takes a lot of preparatory work. If you have colleagues at other schools who have already created a program, or work within a program, get help from them. Ask if you can have a copy of the documents they created and if you can use them to help you build your program. Use the resources on the AASL Web site, specifically the *AASL Learning Standards & Common Core State Standards Crosswalk* (http://www.ala.org/aasl/standards-guidelines/crosswalk), that will help you match AASL standards to the ones in the Common Core State Standards (CCSS) (American Association of School Librarians 2013). Use a lesson plan approach to outline your whole program. State your program goals and how you will meet them; then break your program goals down into goals for each grade level. This will help you determine what you need to teach in each IL session to meet your overall goals. See Figure 10.1 for an outline.

COLLABORATION IN SERVICE OF INFORMATION LITERACY

Marketing

Putting together your program is the first half of the work. The second half starts with marketing. This is the first foundational piece of the collaboration puzzle. How will you sell your program to the teachers at your school? How will you sell it to administrators? Marketing means that you take the resources of the library to the teachers, figuratively and literally, and teach them how to use the resources in valuable ways. Setting up the resources and waiting for interested users is not enough. Some states are beginning to call their school librarians "teacher librarians" to put emphasis on how important the role of teaching and promotion is to the role of a school librarian. A good school librarian should seek opportunities to show how useful library resources are. Opportunities include faculty meetings, staff development days, or even individual and small group appointments with teachers, principals, parents, and students. If you are not actively marketing and teaching the resources of the library, you are not acting as a good school librarian by today's standards.

You need to offer your services, demonstrate your services, and discuss resources that will help your teachers meet their curricular goals. Give them examples of the many ways you can work with them. Tell them that their students' work will be better if they bring them to the library for instruction. You should offer to create or work with them on creating a library assignment for their big modules and student projects. You may even need to go as far as offering to grade the library component of that assignment. In short, you need to keep your school informed of new resources and new services that you have to offer and be willing to work with teachers at the drop of a hat. Be active and blow your own horn.

Building Professional Relationships

This should help you recruit those first few teachers that you need to start developing an IL program, and it will build your professional relationships with your teachers. This is the second foundational piece of collaborating with your teachers. There is undoubtedly a host of different personalities at your school, and some will be easier to connect with than others. Regardless of their personalities, you can develop a professional relationship with all of your teachers. A professional relationship is based on an ability to work together to reach common curriculum goals no matter what your personal feelings toward each other might be. Teachers must understand that you are interested in helping them meet their goals before they will begin to trust you or come to you for help. If teachers do not want to work with you, it does not matter what you know or what resources you have in the library. So the way you act, talk, and interact with others at your school, your professional behavior, is important to achieving both your goals and the goals of your teachers.

Once your program is established and teachers are willing and want to work with you, then think about expanding your program to the whole school. This is your dream IL instruction program that you worked to develop. Approach the administration, and sell your idea. Discuss your success, and discuss what a successful program will do for the school. This is where you break out the research that shows the importance of IL instruction to the whole school and the improvement the school will see in student test scores (Lance 2002). We will examine this research more closely in Chapter 14.

Knowing the Core Curriculum

The third foundational piece in the collaboration process has to do with knowing what learning goals and activities are going on in the classrooms at your school. Teachers often do not even realize how many of the library's resources can help them with their curricular goals, so they do not know that the library can help them. Knowing what is going on in all the classrooms of your school is probably unrealistic, but we do have a few suggestions to help.

First, get outlines of the weekly/monthly lesson plans from each teacher. Some principals require teachers to submit a basic outline that they may make available to you. Or, if you have built a good professional relationship, you can ask teachers what they will be doing during the upcoming week, or month, and offer to help them. You can also attend the grade level or other team planning meetings with your teachers. This will allow you to know what is going on, and it will put you in a position to provide input during planning stages.

No one can know the whole CCSS or your school's grade-level standards, but keep them handy. Look up the relevant parts of the core before attending planning meetings and while reading over weekly and monthly lesson plans. Relate these curricular goals to library resources and services. Think about what help you can offer your teachers to meet these goals. Time is always tight for a school librarian, but almost any curriculum meeting you can attend is extremely valuable. Time is always tight for your teachers. Your help will save them time. Your teachers should look at you as a valuable consultant for all teaching at your school, and that cannot happen if you are isolated in the library and do not know what teachers are doing in their classrooms. In this way, you will be able to meet your curricular standards while you help your teachers meet theirs.

Relevant Quality Resources and Services

The fourth and final piece of the foundation of cooperation is gathering the best teaching and learning resources for your library. A school librarian should always be looking for the latest teaching and learning trends, technologies, and current practices that are being used successfully in the classroom and the library. The school librarian needs to identify quality resources that support professional development and the curriculum. Then within budgetary constraints, a school librarian makes decisions about what to purchase and how best to use the new resource effectively. This is something that the regular classroom teachers do not have the time, money, or expertise to do. Some suggestions to help in this endeavor are reading professional journals to stay current in teaching and learning resources, and library trends and resources, attending training opportunities, and joining state and national organizations pertaining to school libraries, teaching, and learning in general.

The CCSS and other standards go beyond mere support of teaching. They include the ideas of independent learning, exploring, and developing a love of reading. Resources that encourage students to explore their own interest and read for the sake of enjoying a good story need to be purchased for the library in addition to those that support the curriculum and professional development. These other resources will build student use of the library and help develop lifelong learners and readers who will grow up to be library supporters.

Now take a final look at the four foundational pieces of collaboration, marketing, professional relationships, knowledge of teaching activities and curricular goals in each classroom, and gathering the best resources. Are you strong in all four areas? If you are weak in one or two areas, will the collaboration foundation work? Examine your skills, goals, and practices regarding collaboration to see where you can improve and make the foundation strong and functional at your school.

IL instruction should be a big part of what you do. A good IL program requires the cooperation of the teachers and administrators at your school. Therefore, a good program needs to be well organized and planned. A good program will not only promote your services but help your teachers with their instruction, provide students with useful IL skills, and promote academic achievement. This is why library instruction is such an important feature of your reference and library services.

LESSON PLANNING

A lesson plan is an outline of what you want to teach and how you are going to teach it during an instruction session. The outline should include the standard you want to address, how you will address it, and how you will know if you succeeded in addressing it. You can get sample lesson plans from many Web sites. The Library of Congress has a searchable list of lesson plans for teachers (http://www.loc.gov/teachers/). Each lesson plan shows you which standards are meet from a number of standards, including AASL and CCSS ("Teacher Resources" 2013). The AASL has a list of IL lesson plans based on its *Standards for the 21st-Century Learner* (http://aasl.jesandco.org/). You can use its *Crosswalk* to match its standards to the CCSS (http://www.ala .org/aasl/guidelinesandstandards/commoncorecrosswalk). Figure 10.1 shows an outline of the information elements that make up the AASL lesson plans ("AASL Learning4Life Lesson Plan Database" 2013). Use this outline to create your lesson plan and then share it with others.

Start by working with the teacher and developing an assignment. Next, you should move to the end of the process and look at the assignment in terms of what IL standards you can address with these students. If there is little or no involvement on the part of the teacher, then start with the standard and develop an assignment to meet the students' needs and your standards. Keep in mind the amount of time you will have to meet with the students so you do not try to do too much. Keep the standards to a minimum and the resources to a handful.

The outline builds in ideas like modeling, independent practice, and reflection. This is a good reminder to use active learning in your instruction. Problem-based learning is a good method of engaging students. You set up a scenario, and the students have to find the information that will be the solution to this problem in a set amount of time. Authentic learning uses the idea that the active learning you engage the students with should be something that they will encounter and need to know in their real lives.

Assessment can be the most difficult part of lesson planning and teaching. How do you know if the students learned what you wanted them to learn? The time you are planning the assignment with the teacher at the beginning of the process is when you need to plan how to assess student learning. What will their final project be, and how will it be graded? Think about the IL goals you want to teach. How will you find evidence of them in the student projects? Perhaps it is the type and number of resource used, or proper quoting and citing of sources. This kind of assessment is called summative assessment. It summarizes student learning.

Figure 10.1. Lesson Plan Outline

Title

Created By:
Title/Role:
Organization/School Name:
Location:
Grade Level:
Type of Lesson:
Type of Schedule:
Collaboration Continuum:
Content Area:
Content Topic:

Standards

AASL	CCSS
Skills Indicator(s):	
Dispostion Indicator(s):	

Scenario:

Overview:

Final Product:

Library Lesson:

Estimated Lesson Time:

Assessment

Product:
Process:
Self Questioning:

Instructional Plan

Resources students will use:
Interactive Resource URL:
Resources instructor will use:
Other instructor resources:

Instruction/Activities

Direct instruction:
Modeling and guided practice:
Independent practice:
Sharing and reflecting:

Have you taught this lesson before:

Strategies for differentiation:

A second type of assessment is called formative. You should build in moments in your instruction where you stop and ask if the students understand the concept you just discussed. If not, then you need to come up with another example, and if they do, then you can move on. Formative assessment is informal. The intent is for you to learn if you need to modify your instruction to suit student needs and abilities. It is also known as one-minute assessment, because it should not take any longer than that to get qualitative feedback from the students about how the instruction is going. Finally, ask the teacher to assess your instruction session. Peer assessment is a great way to see where you can improve your teaching. Remember, the feedback is not personal, not about you, but about attitudes and behaviors that you can change.

Lastly, ask questions, and ask for questions. This is another way to get feedback from your students and see the real challenges that they are having. You are also modeling behaviors you want your students to do: ask questions, and receive answers. Take every instruction session as an opportunity to promote your reference services. Encourage your students to ask you for help and to ask you questions about anything. You are a professional question answerer after all.

Vocabulary

active learning

assessment

authentic learning

behaviorism

blended classroom

cognitivism

constructivism

flipped classroom

formative assessment

humanism

IL instruction

IL program

instructional style

learning management system

learning theories

lesson plan

marketing

problem-based learning

professional relationships

summative assessment

Questions

How many of the six behavioral guidelines for reference librarians are applicable to an instruction setting?

What is the difference between a formative and a summative assessment? Give an example of each.

How is a learning management system used in a blended classroom environment?

Do you think the analogy of a teacher as an actor on stage is a valid and helpful one?

Is the flipped classroom here to stay or just a trend?

Assignment

Use the outline of a lesson plan in Figure 10.1 and create library instruction session on the topic of your choosing for the grade of your choosing. All aspects of instruction need to be considered and the form completely filled out. Use the AASL lesson plan Web site to help you fill in all the information.

Chapter 11

Creating Library Guides and Web Resources

LIBRARY GUIDES

A library resource is everything a library has purchased and provided access to for its customers. A library guide is a resource created by the librarian to help customers use library resources on their own. A map of the library presented as a one-page handout is a library guide. Its purpose is to show students where things are and how library resources are arranged and to help them find the resources they need. Other examples of library guides would show students how to use the library catalog to find books or how to find magazine articles by searching a database.

Library guides can be general like maps and lists of library services or focused on one particularly helpful feature of a database. No matter the topic, library guides should be short, one-page front and back should be the limit. Library guides are *not* substitutes for instruction, or reference services. They should not be handed out in place of these services, and you should not overwhelm students with them. One library guide at a time is enough. Library guides should be thought of as supplemental materials, as a takeaway from an instruction session used to remind students of what was taught. As a school librarian, you need to notice and even anticipate where students and teachers might need help with library resources and then prepare guides to help them.

Library guides do not need to be printed. You can place digital copies on you library Web site, making them available anytime and from anywhere. This would be a great help to students accessing library resources from home. You can make library guides interactive and create tutorials that students can use whenever they need. Your library Web site should contain library guides like this, and they are not difficult to produce.

TYPES OF LIBRARY GUIDES

Library guides may be informational, like a map or list of library services. They may be bibliographic, instructional, or any combination of the other three. We have discussed bibliographies before. We know that bibliographies have been around a long time. They were once the primary tool for library research and electronic resources have superseded them. Bibliographies never disappeared. We have changed what we call them. Web sites often contain links to other resources. Some Web sites consist only of links to other Web resources and arrange the links by topic. Some library guides contain selected resources to show students what is available to them. Databases are collections of resources. These are examples of the modern bibliography.

Bibliographic Guides

As a library guide, a bibliography serves as an introduction to a topic and as a guide to the resources you have in your collection. If your students consistently show an interest in airplanes, then you should create a bibliographic library guide to your resources on airplanes. You should list on a single sheet of paper the top resources you have on airplanes. It should not be everything you own but a good representation of the types of resources you have. The guide will put your students in the right locations to find other resources. You may arrange the resources by the history and development of the airplane, how planes work, and how to fly a plane. Keep it short, so it will be read. Your guide is a starting point. You want students to ask you for more information and help when they have a question, because this allows you to determine how well they are doing and the type of help you need to give them. Now, every time a student asks you about airplanes, you have a guide that will help him or her get started. You have a teachable moment where you can show the student how to use the guide, where the resources are, get him or her started, and remind him or her that you are there to help with any questions he or she has. After all, you are the ultimate guide.

Instructional and Combination Guides

Instructional and combination library guides may cover any topic, resource, or feature of a resource. You will be engaged in creating a number of these for your students and teachers. Keep them concise. These types of guides lend themselves well to the inclusion of pictures, illustration, and, if created online, media.

It is harder to keep an instructional guide short and maintain clarity, because there is often more information to be covered or many steps to be spelled out. For example, if you write an instructional guide on how to use an electronic resource like *MAS Ultra* or *SIRS*, you would have to be very brief to cover just the most important features. Use your lesson plan as an outline for your instructional guide. This will help you keep your goals and standards in mind, while helping you stay focused on the topic. Even if your guide is to supplement your lecture, demonstration, and hands-on time, using your lesson plan will help you determine what materials and instruction would be valuable to that end. You may need to create a print instructional guide to hand out to your students. Depending on the students' ages and abilities, they may prefer to have a hard copy. However, instructional guides lend themselves well to the electronic environment.

You can create screencast recordings for your instructional guide. A screencast is a video recording of what is on your computer's monitor. For example, you can have your Web page displayed, and the screencasting software will record what happens as you navigate from your home page to a resource, perform a search, and format the results in APA format. The software will also record your narration as you describe why you are doing what you are doing. There are some good free screencasting tools to accomplish this, such as CamStudio for Windows (http://camstudio.org) and Jing for Mac or Windows (http://www.jingproject.com). The freeware does not often include editing features. This means you need to plan what you want to show. You should not worry about making mistakes, acknowledge them with a comment or joking remark, and keep going. The mistakes will humanize you. If you make a lot of mistakes or a big mistake, consider it a practice run and start again. Camtasia for Windows (http://techsmith.com/camtasia.asp) and SnapzPro for Mac (http://www.ambrosiasw.com/utilities/snapzprox) are examples of commercial screen capture products. Each of these tools has tutorials and help files on its Web site that will help you learn how to use its products.

There are many resources to help you with your screencasts. Lists of software are easily googled. *Online Tutorials* at Library Success (http://www.libsuccess .org/index.php?title=Online_Tutorials) offers a list of good tutorials, some basic advice, and a list of software ("Online Tutorials" 2010). The Wikipedia has charts that list screencasting software by price, release date, and features ("Comparison of Screencasting Software" 2013), which can be very helpful when it comes to selecting a software package. TechHive has a short guide with tips to get you started with screencasting (Daw 2012).

Another resource for creating instructional guides is called *Guide on the Side* (http://code.library.arizona.edu/gots/). It is free but needs to be set up on a Linux server. Your district technologist may have to do this for you. Once it is set up, you access a Web address to get to the software and create and publish your guides. Guide on the Side splits the screen into two parts. The main screen is a live Web page, like your library home page. In a column on the left-hand side is the "guide." In this space, you can put text, images, definitions, and questions. This allows you to write an instruction, include an image of what you want the students to do, and then ask them to do it. The students perform your instruction in the live window and then advance the instruction window. Guide on the Side also allows you to include self-answering questions that provide instant feedback to the students, or you can choose to create a graded quiz. With this option, students do not receive any feedback other than a grade, and you receive information about who took the quiz and his or her grade. This is our way of tracking who completed a tutorial.

Your electronic guides are Web pages. If you do not feel comfortable creating Web pages, there are many services available to help you. Google sites (http://sites.google.com/) or Weebly (http://www.weebly.com/) make it easy to create a Web site with multiple Web pages or a Wiki for free. You can link to your new Web site from you library page or have these be your library pages. Another service called LibGuides (http://springshare.com/libguides/) helps you create library guides. This is not a free service, but the price is not too high. It may be a resource best purchased and maintained at the district level.

LibGuides allows you to create Web pages with a consistent look, arrangement, and information elements. A consistent look helps to brand your library and makes it easier for customers to use the guides you created. They will know where to look for specific kinds of information. Because libguides pages are Web pages, you can include embedded videos, podcasts, chat reference box, links to library resources, and so on, along with your text describing resources or services. Another great feature of LibGuides is that it collects usage information. LibGuides is used by many libraries, has an active user group that can provide examples, and helps in creating your own guides. LibGuides users have posted many examples of the guides they have created (http://bestof.libguides.com/home) (Springshare 2013). Even if you decided not to use the program, you can look at the examples and use the ideas you find there to help create your guides.

Branding your library guides may sound like you need to develop a library logo and slogan, but you do not have to do that. Branding is about consistent messaging. An interesting study on academic library handouts is a case in point. The findings showed that 83 percent of these handouts were in support of traditional research papers and did not support any other form of project. Worse yet, they focused on the properties of the research paper and not on resources. Add to that the fact that students use guides to help them define the context in which they are operating and "how to find and use appropriate information sources and develop a course-related research strategy" (Head and Eisenberg 2010a), which they are not getting from these guides. Most of the guides in the study referred to print resources over electronic resources, 60 percent to 43 percent, an oddity because electronic is so popular and prevalent at the college level where the guides were from. Finally, only 13 percent of these guides mentioned consulting a librarian.

Every one of your guides should mention consulting a librarian for more help and list all the ways you can be contacted. The Web versions of your guides should include links to your e-mail and chat or even include a live chat box, even if you make a point of mentioning your reference services in every instruction session you do. Your library hours and any other basic library information should be included. A consistent look and feel makes your guides easier to navigate and brands these resources that you created.

Library guides may become a management issue. The more you create, the more you have to maintain and update. If you change the look and arrangement of your library home page, you may need to change a graphic on most of your library guides. Using a service like LibGuides will make the management of your library guides easier by having them all in one place and being able to make universal changes. For example, all of your guides may use a link to the same image of your library home page. When you change your Web page, a new image using the same file name can be substituted, and all of those links will display the new image. Another idea is not to create separate print and electronic versions of your library guides; instead, maintain only your electronic versions and print them when hard copies are needed.

WEB PRESENCE 2.0

You can also use your Web site to display a calendar of upcoming library events and trainings, host a discussion blog, list new resources, and reach out to students, teachers, and even parents to use and contribute to the success of the library. Your Web site connects your customers to all the wonderful resources, services, and guides you have created. Your Web site is a great tool to reach students, teachers, and even parents. It can be used to keep your customers informed about library goings-on, and aside from you, it is your best marketing tool. These are social media tools.

Blogs are Web sites that give your users the ability to post their messages in response to an initial post created by you. This is a useful way to get input from all customers on any topic. A blog would not replace your library Web site but could be a link from your home page or even occupy a column on your home page. Ask around your school district to see if help is available in adding a blog to your Web site, or use one of such free blog tools as WordPress.com (http://wordpress.com/), or Blogger (http://www.blogger.com), which is now part of the suite of services Google offers. There are tutorials available at the site to help with the account set up and blog creation. Once your blog is created, you can link to it from your library Web site. You will have a choice to have an open blog or require a password that you can give out before users are allowed to post.

Microblogging is exemplified by Twitter (http://twitter.com/). Twitter is one of the most popular Web sites in the world. Microblogs, like Twitter, are used to post short messages of no more than 140 characters, which answers the question, "What are you doing, now?" It is a way to keep in touch with and update your friends on what is going on. Twitter accounts have followers. Friends can subscribe to your account, and each time you post a message, they are notified. You can also display your Twitter posts on your library home page. This makes it easy for students to see what you have been doing on Twitter and makes them aware that you are offering this service.

Wikis are another tool that you might want to be part of your library Web presence. In a Wiki, anyone can create, edit, and add to a post. This makes Wikis a good tool to use when you want a group of people to work together on a learning activity. Wikipedia is the most famous Wiki (http://wikipedia.org) and is an open, ongoing encyclopedia creation project where virtually anyone can post, delete, change, and create new entries and otherwise participate in the creation of this online encyclopedia. An automatic history of all entries, deletions and changes to a document, and who made them are maintained. This enables you to restore any document to a previous state at any time, track participation, and deal with malicious activity.

Examples of good projects for Wikis include the following: planning activities between teachers and others where they are giving suggestions, making lists, or otherwise attempting to come up with a plan as a group; creating a list of definitions on such topics as an online dictionary of terms for a class; or having a group working on a common document they all need to access and edit. There are several Wiki sites that will allow you to create your own Wikis for free, including WikiSpaces (http://wikispaces.com) and PBWorks (http://pbworks.com/).

Facebook (https://www.facebook.com/) is the most recognizable social media site. A student needs to be 13 years old to have a Facebook account. If you work in an elementary or a middle school, creating an account there would not reach your customers. You can use your Facebook account with high school students to keep them informed of library activities and services. Your posts to Facebook can be automatically sent out as your Twitter post, which makes this option a great way to support two services, though you would not be taking full advantage of the features of either. Facebook allows you to post pictures and media. Students can friend your library and follow what you are doing.

Another interesting social media site is Pinterest (https://pinterest.com/), which is based on the idea of collecting pictures, list, and other items and pinning them to a bulletin board. Pinterest has grown to be the 40th most popular site in the world and the 13th most popular in the United States (Alexa 2013b). You can create Pinterest boards for library programs or student projects. You could create a board outlining a student assignment and then post the completed assignments there as well.

YouTube (http://www.youtube.com/) is another popular social media site. You can have your own YouTube channel where you post all of the videos that you have created. Students can subscribe to your channel, and you can post student videos to your channel. You can place a link to your channel on your library home page. This makes all of your videos easily accessible in one place.

There is a health sciences library in Alabama that maintains in addition to its Web site a Facebook account, a Pinterest account, a Twitter account, a YouTube account, and six blogs. The librarians at this library concluded that it was worth their time to maintain all of these contact points with their customers (Vucovich et al. 2013). You will not want to do that. You do need to decide if you want to get involved with a social media service. You know that social media is a great way to reach your customers and is an excellent marketing tool. You know you can use these resources to promote library services, create workspaces for student projects, and develop tutorials. You need to decide what you can or cannot maintain.

You cannot simply create a Facebook or Twitter account. You have to post to your account at least once a week. If you do not keep feeding information to your account, it will become stale. Students and teachers will have no reason to visit it. You need a plan to keep your social media accounts fed with new information. A survey of high school libraries around Ogden, Utah, found that each high school had only one librarian, and most had only one part-time assistant. Some had no assistants (Christensen, Morgan, and Kinikin 2013). You may need to recruit student employees/volunteers to help you with your social media program. They can take pictures and videos and given guidelines and a topic may even be able to help you with your posts. You should also model good information behavior in your use of these resources by citing your sources and not violating copyright.

Figure 11.1. Basic Library Guide

Pine Hollow Elementary User Guide # 1
Guide to the Library

Library Hours

Monday	9:00 am – 12:00 noon,	1:00 pm – 5:00 pm
Tuesday	9:00 am – 12:00 noon,	1:00 pm – 5:00 pm
Wednesday	9:00 am – 12:00 noon,	1:00 pm – 3:00 pm
Thursday	9:00 am – 12:00 noon,	1:00 pm – 5:00 pm
Friday	9:00 am – 12:00 noon,	1:00 pm – 3:00 pm

> Need help answering a question, or finding materials, or using the computer?
> Ask the librarians at the Reference/Circulation desk!
> Or call 555-rfnc.

Circulation: Bring your materials to check out to the Reference/Circulation desk.
Books check out for two weeks.
Magazines and DVDs check out for one week.
Reference books must be used in the library.

Books are arranged using the Dewey Decimal System.
Magazines are arranged alphabetically.

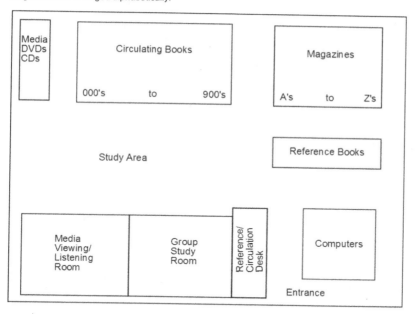

Social media, guide, or tutorial software will require time to learn, implement, and use. Choose the ones you are going to use carefully. After a set period of time, evaluate the success of using these services. These services track usage of your pages. Use this information to help you in your evaluation. Do not go by anecdotal information or a gut feeling. Although numbers may not be the whole picture, they are easy to understand and can impress school administrators. Did these services help you with your marketing and instruction? Are they

Figure 11.2. SIRS Discoverer Biography Guide

Pine Hollow Elementary User Guide # 13
How to Find Biographies Using SIRS Discoverer

The SIRS Biographies has almost 2000 biographies of famous people. You should be able to find information on just about anyone who is famous from "Michael Jordan" to "Mark Twain."

Here's How:

1. Double Click on the "**SIRS Discoverer**" icon on any library computer. Then select "**Biographies**" from the list in the right hand column.
2. The Biographies screen appears with an Alphabetical browse.
3. Select the first letter of the LAST NAME of the person whose biography you want to view.

A B C D E F G

4. Select a name from the list to view a list of article titles.

DiCaprio, Leonardo
Dickens, Charles
Dickinson, Emily
Diemer, Walter E.
DiMaggio, Joe
Dion, Celine
Disney, Walt
Dix, Dorthea

Database Features

- Science Fair Explorer
- Skills Discoverer
- Activities
- Biographies
- Fiction
- Country Facts Updated!
- Pictures
- Maps of the World
- Educators' Resources
- Dictionary / Thesaurus

Sort by: [Title | Publication | Lexile | Date] ▲ ▼   Details: [Show | Hide]

1. ■ 75 Years of Mickey 🔲 📷 P
   KRT OnePages: Nov. 7, 2003; Lexile Score: 1080; 13K.
   Summary: Mickey Mouse turns 75 in 2003. "[B]ut you'd never know it by looking at him. Mickey Mo the Disney empire—the three-circle silhouette of his head is one of the most recognized corporate syr the creator of Mickey Mouse. Mickey's friends, his milestones and his movies are described
   Descriptors: Mickey Mouse (Cartoon character), Walt Disney Company, Animators, Anniversaries, C

2. ■ Walt Disney 🔲 📷 a P
   Famous Faces from Time: 2001; Lexile Score: 1100; 6K
   Summary: Walt Disney "created the world's most popular mouse" (*Famous Faces from Time*) Lea
   Descriptors: Mickey Mouse (Cartoon character), Motion picture producers and directors, Animators.

3. ■ Walt Disney (1901-1966) 🔲 📷 P
   SIRS Discoverer: Fall 1996; Lexile Score: 950; 6K.
   Summary: Walter Elias Disney was born on December 5, 1901, in Chicago, Illinois. He became one
   Descriptors: Amusement parks, Motion picture producers and directors, Disney, Walt (1901-1966)

> Need help answering a question, or finding materials, or using the computer?
> Ask the librarians at the Reference/Circulation desk!
> Or call 555-rfnc.

being used by your students, teachers, and/or parents? Has it been a good investment of time and effort, or should you consider a different service or no service at all? You may need to think outside the box to use them in ways that engage your students, teachers, and parents. New technologies will help you create new services and resources. The benefits of using social media often outweigh the efforts needed to maintain them.

EXAMPLES

Figures 11.1 and 11.2 show two examples we created for a fictional school, Pine Hollow Elementary. The first is an informational guide to a library. It is a map to the library. Its purpose is to provide an overview of where the library's collections are located and to give students basic information about the library.

The next library guide is an instructional guide that shows the elementary students how to find biographical information using SIRS Discoverer. This guide illustrates the steps to take to find information about a famous person.

Vocabulary

bibliographic guide	marketing
blog	microblogging
branding	screencasting
combination guide	social media
informational guide	tutorial
instructional guide	Wiki

Questions

Do you think the example library guides are good ones? Are they doing what they are supposed to? What changes would you make?

If you had time to maintain only one social media source, which one would it be and why?

How old do students need to be to use an electronic library guide well without any print guide available?

Is branding a valid concept for an elementary, a middle, or a high school library?

Assignment

Create a library guide to accompany your lesson plan from Chapter 10.

Pick a social media platform and then use it to promote a library story hour for students and their parents, a database training for teachers, and library resources on the Civil War for use in school-wide projects.

Chapter **12**

Searching for Information

There are many, many electronic resources available for use. In this chapter we examine database basics and how search works. These concepts have broad application across databases. The focus of this chapter is on vendor-supplied databases, those commercial resources you buy on behalf of your students. Many of these resources are purchased on your behalf by the state, county, or school district for use in the school library. This chapter will help you instruct your students and teachers in the effective use of your library's electronic resources.

WHAT IS A DATABASE?

Electronic resources are databases of information. Databases store information and provide a means to retrieve it. The standard means of storing information in a database is a record. A record consists of fields. Each field is a container for a specific type of data. Here is a sample list of fields:

Author

Title of the article

Name of journals

Publication information

Subject headings

Abstract

Each individual field has little value without the other. Taken together, the data in fields provide information about one item in the database. The fields listed here comprise standard information found in a database of magazine and journal articles. With the exception of the author field, these fields represent required information. You cannot have a record that just has the title of an article and nothing else. Other fields may be included in a database that each contain specific information. This is how databases impose a structure on the information they collect and how they enable searching.

Can a printed reference resource be a database? For example, look closely at a dictionary. It is easy to see the structure used to organize the information into a record. A record is all the information associated with a word. The fields are the headword (the word being defined), part of speech, pronunciation, definition, and so on. All the records together make up the database that is the dictionary.

SEARCHING AN ELECTRONIC RESOURCE

The structured information in a database helps make finding information in the database easier. If you have used a database program like Microsoft Access, you know that you use a query or a report to extract the information that fits your criteria. In a database provided by a vendor, Google, or Bing, we use search engines to extract the information we need.

Many years ago when electronic resources were new, and computers were expensive, there was a debate about establishing a standardized search language. If every vendor used the standard language, you would only have to learn one search language, and with only one language to learn, you could learn it well. You would be able to search any database efficiently and effectively.

The benefits of using the standard search language were obvious, but it never happened. Database vendors had no interest in it. Instead, they had a vested interest in promoting their own search engines with their own search languages. Companies put a lot of time and money into developing their own search engines. It differentiated their product from their competitors, which was important since they could be searching the same database of material. Some of the earliest databases were produced by the government, like Medline and ERIC. These databases were available to any vendor. Therefore, you could get the same information from multiple vendors, which meant that vendors had to differentiate their products through their search engines and optional features.

However, there was a basic set of commands and concepts that were fundamental to all database searching, and that has not changed. This has led to search engines that are far more similar than they are divergent. Commands are the language of the search. They comprise the mechanical aspect of searching. In addition, there are the words you choose to enter in the search engine. We will call those words the search terms or keywords. Search mechanics and search terms are further subdivided, and each subdivision will be analyzed in the following sections.

SEARCH MECHANICS

Search mechanics are the commands the search engine software interprets, and how it interprets them to execute a search. They are the language of the search engines—as opposed to the language used in the search. They have their own vocabulary and grammar. Whatever you enter into a search box is the search statement. It is what the search engine processes and parses to execute a search. The search engine looks for command words like Boolean operators to tell it what to do.

Boolean Logic and Venn Diagrams

Boolean logic is the fundamental principle behind most search engines. There are three Boolean operators, which are also called logical operators. They were developed by George Boole (1815–1864), an English mathematician who pioneered mathematical logic (Gillispie 1970a).

The Boolean operators are the following:

- AND
- OR
- NOT

The operators do not have to be in upper case, but we will write them this way to make them easier to see in the text of this book.

Venn diagrams are used to illustrate how Boolean operators work. They were developed by John Venn (1834–1923), who was also an English mathematician (Gillispie 1970b). Venn diagrams consist of overlapping circles with appropriate areas shaded to represent the application of a Boolean operator on search terms and search sets. You will see them in Figure 12.1.

AND

AND is the most important and useful of the Boolean operators. It is the operator of intersection. It finds where search terms overlap and narrows search results. If you are searching a database and want to find all the articles that mention both "Facebook" and "anxiety," you use AND. The search statement is:

Facebook AND anxiety

The Venn diagram for this search is:

Numbers may help explain how AND works. For example, you search a database and find 1,000 articles about Facebook. You then do a new search and find 500 articles about anxiety. When you search for "Facebook AND anxiety," you

Figure 12.1. AND Operator

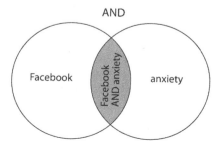

Figure 12.2. AND Operator with Three Terms

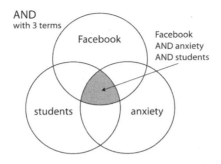

find 40 articles. These 40 articles represent the only articles in your database that mention both of your search terms. This is the intersection of your ideas.

You may use multiple ANDs in your search. Each AND reduces the number of articles you find. This is a great way to refine your search and to narrow the focus of your topic. For example, if we add a third search term, students, to our search statement, it would change our search to:

Facebook AND anxiety AND students

The Venn diagram now becomes more complicated. Figure 12.2 shows the Venn diagram for two ANDs.

Instead of finding 40 articles, this time the search retrieves only 12. These 12 articles may better reflect the intent of your search and be more relevant. Relevance versus retrieval reflects a basic concern when searching and a problem for search engine designers. In general, the higher your retrieval of items, the lower your relevance, and the higher your relevance of items retrieved, the lower your retrieval. For example, you are interested in the effect that Facebook usage has on the anxiety levels of high school students, and your search statement is Facebook.

This search would result in very high retrieval and very low relevance. "False hits" is the terminology used to describe the results that are not relevant to the search. Using our first example search statement of "Facebook AND anxiety" would lower the retrieval significantly while also increasing the relevance of the retrieved articles significantly. However, as the relevance rises and the retrieval lowers, the likelihood that relevant items will be eliminated from the results also increases.

For example, if we had searched for "Facebook AND anxiety AND depression AND boys AND high school," the results, if there are any, would be highly relevant. However, we may have cut out the perfect articles, because one article studied both boys and girls using the term "students," another used the term "teenagers" never mentioning high school, and a third talked about anxiety disorders, but did not directly say "depression." In this case, we have "missed hits," positive results that have been eliminated by a narrow search.

Search engine designers look for ways of increasing relevance without adversely impacting retrieval. Some of these methods are examined later in this chapter. As a searcher, you need to be aware of this phenomenon and seek a balance between relevance and retrieval in your searches. This concept may be too much for many students to understand, but you can present the idea as narrowing and broadening search results based on how many items were retrieved by the search. One hundred items are too many; you will need to narrow your search. Four items are too few; you will need to broaden your search.

OR

OR is the Boolean operator of union. It increases the number of items retrieved by your search. It broadens your search. If you are searching a database and want to find all the articles that mention either "Facebook" or "anxiety," you use OR. The search statement is:

Facebook OR anxiety

The Venn diagram for this search is shown in Figure 12.3.

In our example database, there are 1,000 items that mention "Facebook" and 500 that mention "anxiety." How many articles meet the search criteria? The search found 1,460 articles, not 1,500. We have 40 articles in our database that mention both Facebook and anxiety. The search for "Facebook" includes those 40 articles. The search for "anxiety" also includes those 40 items. If you add these numbers together, you would be counting the overlap twice. The OR search counts the overlap only once.

The OR operator would not be used in a search with these search terms. The OR operator does not find a relationship between the search terms. The AND operator shows a relationship by finding the interaction of the terms. To use OR effectively, the terms, the ideas you link together with OR, should be related to one another, or synonyms. For example, "Facebook OR Twitter OR Pinterest" links together these related items as a search for "social media sites."

NOT

NOT is the Boolean operator of exclusion. It decreases the number of items retrieved and narrows your search by eliminating a term from the results. If you are searching a database and want to find all the articles that mention "Facebook" but do not mention "anxiety," you use NOT. The search statement is:

Facebook NOT anxiety

The Venn diagram for this search is shown in Figure 12.4.

Figure 12.3. OR Operator

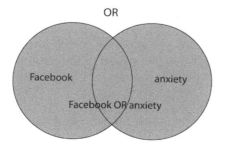

Figure 12.4. NOT Operator

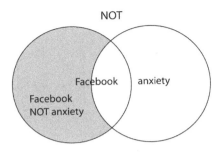

For example, you know that there are 1,000 articles about Facebook in our database and 500 articles about anxiety. A search for "Facebook NOT anxiety" will find 960 articles. You know this because your AND search for those terms found 40 articles that overlapped. NOT eliminates the second term and, therefore, the overlap between the two terms.

NOT is the hardest, and the most specialized, of the Boolean operators to use effectively. It is used to improve the relevance of your search by eliminating ideas you do not want in your search. You want to search for students, but you do not want to include "college students" in your search results. You can search for "students NOT college" to eliminate that idea from your search and improve your search's relevance.

Proximity and Phrase Searching

Searches composed of only Boolean operators can be quite effective and efficient. Even so, false hits are commonplace, especially when searching large databases or searching the full text. Many databases contain the full text of the information sources. For example, an article database's content may be 60 percent full text, with the other 40 percent of the content having only an abstract. A newspaper database's content may be 100 percent full text, which means that every item in the database represents the full article from the newspaper. While many databases are largely constructed of full-text items, most databases do not default to a full-text search. The search engine searches only a select set of fields, such as author, title of the article, name of the journal, subject terms, and abstract. If you wish to actually search the entire content of the items in the database, you have to choose to do a full-text search.

Proximity and phrase searching improve the relevance of your search and are extremely useful search tools. They are also extremely limiting. In a proximity search, a word is searched for in relation to another word. Proximity operators are not used that often anymore. One problem with proximity operators is that they are not standardized across vendor platforms. Each vendor has its own implementation of proximity. You will need to check the help screen in the database to find how proximity is implemented in the database you are searching.

Here is an example of what a proximity search may look like:

bears N/5 Utah

This search looked for the word "bears," and "bears" had to be within five words of the word "Utah." The assumption with proximity searching is that close proximity implies strong relationship. Because "bears" was found close to "Utah," the articles retrieved should be focused on "Utah bears," as opposed to Wyoming or Montana bears, though they have not been excluded from the search. The number of words that come between the search terms can be changed by changing the number in the operator: N/8 would allow up to eight words, while N/2 would allow only two words.

Proximity operators can also require that the search terms occur in a specific order. In the earlier example, "bears" could show up on either side of the word "Utah." If we change the operator to a W/5, then we are telling the search engine to find "bears" within five words before "Utah."

There are many proximity operators. The search engine you are using will determine which ones are available to you. There are proximity operators that require the search terms to be in the same field as each other, within the same sentence, or within the same paragraph. There may be two sets of these operators for those terms: one for order and one for no order.

Phrase searching is much less complicated than proximity search, and the phrase operator is largely the same across databases and even Web search engines. The phrase operator is the double quotation mark. Anything enclosed in quotes is searched for exactly as typed. Assume you have a student who wants to find information about a specific breed of dog. You could construct the search as:

fox AND terriers

However, you can see that there will be a number of false hits. You can use proximity to improve your search:

fox W/2 terriers

But a phrase search is the most appropriate and effective:

"fox terriers"

That search will find only articles that mention "fox terriers." Phrase searching is an ideal way to search for multiword phrases that convey one idea. For example, "Bryce Canyon National Park" is the phrase that represents one specific place, and "information behavior" represents an idea. A phrase search is essentially a proximity search with order:

fox W/0 terriers

Proximity and phrase searching are powerful tools, with phrase searching being the preferred method. These search operators are much more limiting than AND. Care needs to be taken when using them. The longer the phrase is, the fewer items that will be retrieved. This raises the number of missed hits. Phrases should be a unique representation of an idea. For example, you do not want to search for the phrase "California laws" since that idea can also be expressed as "laws of California" or "California state laws," or even as "California code."

Truncation and Wildcards

Web search engines do a wonderful job looking for alternate spellings and plurals of the search terms we enter. Vendor search engines were not this sophisticated in the past, and you needed to use special operators to enable this kind of searching. Now these search engines also automatically search for plurals and alternate spellings. They are just not as good at it as the Web search engines, yet.

Truncation describes the process of finding word endings on a truncated term. The asterisk (*) is widely accepted as the truncation symbol in vendor databases. For example, you can search for: change*. The asterisk will find any word ending, including no word ending, that can be placed on "change" and make sense. This search would yield: change, changes, changed, changeling, or changeable. As you can see, the asterisk performs an OR search. If your truncation looked like this: chang*, the search would also yield "changing." Truncation does not find synonyms. Our search for change* will not find "alter" or "modify." It finds only word endings.

Truncation is also known as right-hand truncation because you truncate on the right side of the word. Left-hand truncation is very rare. It is simply not necessary in most searches. However, it is implemented in the electronic version of the *Oxford English Dictionary*. Left-hand truncation allows you to search for the words that end in "gry," for instance, which is a big help to librarians who have to answer that question.

Wildcards are used to find alternate spellings of a word. A classic example is: colo?r. This search is the equivalent of: color OR colour. The question mark is the wildcard symbol. It tells the search engine to find either zero or one other letter that makes sense in this context. The only other letter that works is the letter "u," which gives us the British spelling "colour." Vendor databases are handling this alternate spelling without the need for using the wildcard operator. However, a more esoteric example navajo/navaho stumps the search engine and requires the use of a wildcard in such a search as nava?o. In most cases, wildcards will not be necessary anymore.

Truncation and wildcard operators are not standardized. You would need to consult the help screen from the database vendor to see which characters it uses for these operators. The need for these operators is dwindling, but they may still be necessary to improve a search. You need to be aware of them, but their value to students is very limited.

Order of Execution and Nesting

Order of execution refers to the order in which search engines interpret commands. It may seem like this should not matter, but it does, and it makes a big difference in the search results you retrieve. For example, a student is working with this research question: What impact do genetically modified foods (GMOs) have on insects and birds? The search statement for this research question could look like this:

insects OR birds AND "genetically modified foods" OR GMOs

We understand the intent of the search statement. The search engine does not. It follows rules for interpreting search statements and which commands to execute in what order. In general, search engines will execute AND statements first and then OR. Figure 12.5 shows how the search engine interprets our search.

The results of this search are not what we expected. While "birds AND genetically modified foods" is good, getting everything in the database about

Figure 12.5. Order of Execution

insects OR birds AND "genetically modified foods" OR GMOs
second   first   third

Alternatively:

1. (birds AND "genetically modified foods")
2. OR insects
3. OR GMOs

insects and everything about GMOs is not. Our search is a mess with the relevant material buried within a large number of irrelevant hits. The Venn diagram for this search is in Figure 12.6.

To fix this problem, we need to control the order of execution. One way to do this is to use parentheses. Parentheses tell the database to execute the commands found within them first. This search technique is called nesting. You can see in Figure 12.7 that nesting the operators fixed the problem we had with the order of execution in our search. These results are what we wanted. The Venn diagram in Figure 12.8 further illustrates the success of this search.

This is the Venn diagram for our nested search.

Nesting is an essential concept to understand in order to search effectively. In our example, the parenthetical material in each nest forms a set, and then those two sets are AND'ed together. That is why the Venn diagram for our search looks

Figure 12.6. Search Not Controlled for the Order of Execution

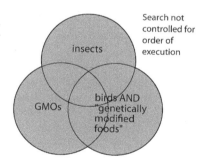

Figure 12.7. Search Statement with Parentheses

(insects OR birds) AND ("genetically modified foods" OR GMOs)
first   second

Alternatively:

1. (insects OR birds)
2. AND ("genetically modified foods" OR GMOs)

Figure 12.8. Search Controlled for the Order of Execution

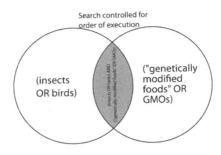

exactly like the Venn diagram for any two-term search. One circle is used for each set.

Set Logic

The Venn diagram in Figure 12.8 is an example of set logic. The advanced search screens on vendor-supplied databases use set logic. We will talk about that more in the next chapter. Using advanced search screens or crafting long searches with parentheses is one way to use set logic. The other method is often buried in the search engine under such a heading as "search history."

Use the previous nesting example, and instead of searching for all the information at once, search only for the idea contained in the first nest or set. Each set should represent one idea and its synonyms. Next, you would search for the second idea contained in the second set, then a third idea, and so on. Now you have the results from multiple searches, but the results are not related to one another. Finally, you combine the sets using the AND operator and the database's designation for the sets. It may look like this:

S1 AND S2 AND S3

Using set logic in this way controls for the order of execution and allows you to restructure your search easily. You can combine, recombine, and add additional sets to your search until you get the results that work best for your information need. This technique works well for searches that seek to combine many ideas. If the search retrieves too few hits, then a set can be dropped from the search to find more hits. If too many items are found, then a set can be added to retrieve fewer but more relevant hits.

Since this search option is usually difficult to locate in a search engine, it is better to use the advanced search screen and teach students how to use each line to create a search set that represents one idea.

SEARCH TERMS

In this chapter, we have so far discussed search mechanics or how search engines work. Now, we will turn our attention to the ideas we wish to find and the words we need to use to find them. Search terms are those words we input into the search engine. Choosing the wrong words can lead to a failed search, whereas choosing the right words can lead to success. How do we choose the terms for search?

Keyword

A keyword is a significant word found in the title and frequently used in the text of a document that represents the content of the whole document ("Keyword [linguistics]" 2013; "Keyword, N." 2013; Merriam-Webster, Inc. 2013c). In Web 2.0 terminology, a keyword is a tag. As a search term, a keyword is a term that, you hope, meets that definition and returns the results you are after. It is a single word, or short phrase, which embodies one of the concepts or ideas that you are searching.

Choosing the right keywords can be difficult for anyone to do. Expect it to be difficult for students who have less experience researching and less knowledge of the subjects they are researching. To help students find keywords, start with the research question. A student wants to find information on junk food and its contribution to weight problems in kids.

Pick out the most important concepts, the biggest ideas that describe this question in the fewest words. You should be left with "junk food," "weight problems," and "kids." These are your keywords. Keywords are often nouns. "Contribution" is not a keyword. It does not further clarify the topic. It has a verb form and can be replaced with words like "effect" and "impact" without changing the meaning of the research question. It is descriptive of the relationship between the keywords, but that relationship will be found through the use of the Boolean AND.

Think of synonyms and alternate ways to express these ideas. "Junk food" is a specific concept. "Fast food" may be considered a subset of "junk food," and a useful synonym can be made for a search. "Snack food" is too broad and has less of a negative implication. Snack food can also be healthy. "Weight problems" could be "obesity," and "kids" could be "children" or "teens." "Weight problems" and "kids" could be "childhood obesity." Now you link the ideas together using AND, and your search statement is:

"junk food" AND "childhood obesity"

Now, the evaluation process takes over. Did this search work well? If not, is there at least one good item on the results list? What keywords did that item use to describe the topic? Does the search need to be refined and tried again? Keyword searching can be difficult, because the best keywords for a topic may not be known. It is important to be flexible, to explore, to evaluate results, and to refine search statements.

Controlled Vocabulary and Subject Search

One way to improve the relevance of your search results is to use controlled vocabulary terms as your search terms. A controlled vocabulary is a list of prescribed subject terms that are used to describe items. These lists of terms correspond to a database and were published in book form in the past. *Thesaurus of ERIC Descriptors* or *Library of Congress Subject Headings* are two examples. Both of these resources list the prescribed subject terms that the indexers at ERIC and catalogers across the country are required to use to describe the

Figure 12.9. ERIC Thesaurus Entry for School Libraries

School Libraries

Category: Information/Communications Systems	
Related Terms	Broader Terms
Learning Resources Centers	Libraries
Librarian Teacher Cooperation	Narrower Terms
Media Specialists	N/A
Schools	Use this term instead of
	Elementary School Libraries (1966 1980) High School Libraries Secondary School Libraries

Added to ERIC: 7/1/1966

article or book they are indexing or cataloging. This method ensures consistency.

When searching a database with a controlled vocabulary term, you should find *all* the items in the database on that topic. For example, you can search for the keyword "fracking" in a database and find many articles. However, if you used the controlled vocabulary term for "fracking," "hydraulic fracturing," you would find all the articles in the database on this topic. The search result would include articles that used only "fracking" to describe this idea and those that used "hydraulic fracturing," because all of the articles would be indexed with the controlled vocabulary term "hydraulic fracturing."

Vendor-supplied database allows you to search in the subject field to exploit the use of controlled vocabulary. You need to find the proper terms to use to make the most of this search. These databases will have links to "subject terms," "thesaurus," or possibly something else. You will need to explore the database you are using to find the controlled vocabulary. Clicking on these links brings up a search box that will allow you to look for the official subject terminology used in that database.

Figure 12.9 shows an entry from the ERIC thesaurus taken from the ERIC Web site (hppt://eric.ed.gov; "School Libraries" 2013). The word(s) in bold print at the top of the entry are the headword. This is what we searched for in the thesaurus, "school libraries" in our example.

Category refers to the broadest subject area to which our term belongs, while broader terms list terms that are a step broader than our original term. There are no terms narrower than "school libraries," though there are a number of related terms listed. These terms, "Elementary School Libraries," "High School Libraries," and "Secondary School Libraries," are not to be used. They are either synonyms for our topic or old terminology that has been replaced. Finally, there is the date when the term was added to the ERIC thesaurus.

Looking up the preferred terminology helps with your search, but the best way to use these terms is to do a subject search. Using "hydraulic fracturing" mentioned earlier, a database was searched twice. The first time, the default search was used. This is a keyword search. It returned 1,530 items. The second time, a subject-term search was used. This time, 1,230 items were found for "hydraulic fracturing." The keyword search found 287 more articles, but in these additional articles, "hydraulic fracturing" is not the focus. "Hydraulic fracturing" is not the subject of the article. The keyword search has higher retrieval, but the subject search has higher relevance.

The best way to perform a subject search is to use the advanced search screen. Drop-down boxes next to the search boxes provide you the choice of fields you want to search. You can select the subject field from this list, and your search will look for your controlled vocabulary terms as subject terms that are assigned to the items in the database by the indexers.

Controlled vocabulary/subject searching is a fast and efficient way to find all the articles on your topic. Another way to perform a subject search without first looking up the preferred term is to do a keyword search, then consult the results list, and select a relevant item. On the record for that item, you will see the subject terms used to describe it. You can use the subject term you want to modify your search, and try again, or you can click on the subject term to perform a new subject search instantly.

Keyword searching is a fine way to search, and it is the best way to search if the terminology of your subject is very recent. Subject searching, on the other hand, ensures more relevant and complete results.

Stop Words

Stop words are words that you cannot find with a search. Stop words, like "and," "or," "not," "with," and "in," are the commands used to tell the search engine what to do. Stop words, like "the," "it," "a," and "an," are short, common words that retrieve too many items if you could search for them. Stop words can be thought of as a subset of the controlled vocabulary. These are the list of prescribed terms that cannot be searched.

FEDERATED SEARCH

Federated searching is fading away, as Web-scale discovery systems move into the technology spot light. A federated search allows customers to search multiple databases across a number of vendors at the same time. There are advantages to this kind of searching. Customers do not have to pick which database is the best for their topic. Good resources that are not first choices will receive more searches and more exposure. Articles, books, eBooks, and media resources can all be searched from a Google-like search box.

The simplified model given in Figure 12.10 shows that a search using a federated search engine is sent to the vendors of the various databases being searched, including the library catalog. The results are returned from the databases to the federated search software that processes the results, removes duplicate information, and displays the results to the customer. The results can be displayed in different manners. The results screen can show the results from each individual database searched, or they can be integrated into one list.

Federated search can be configured to search subsets of your databases. For example, you can set up one federated search for your electronic reference materials, another to search your journal databases, and a third to search all the library catalogs in the area. Another advantage federated searching offers

Figure 12.10. Federated Search Model

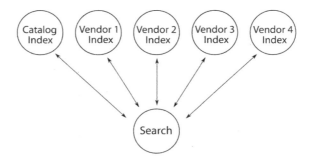

is the ability to give customers results from databases they might not have considered searching or did not even know they had. It is a fast and simple way to search through large amounts of information.

Federated searching has its disadvantages. It introduces errors into your usage statistics, as those little used databases show high numbers of searches that may not reflect actual use of the material in the database. If you have databases that limit the number of customers who can be using them at the same time, federated searching will take up one of those seats. This leads to customers getting false zero results when there are too many customers searching the database at one time. Federated searching is simplified to work with many resources. The unique search abilities of a particular database can be lost. Finally, another argument states that federated searching does not teach the good search skill that students will need in the future, and it even encourages the "good enough" attitude that students learn from using resources like Google (Rethlefsen 2008).

WEB-SCALE DISCOVERY SYSTEMS

Web-scale discovery systems solve some of the problems that federated searching has, like the time they take to broadcast the search, receive the results, and create the display. Web-scale discovery systems can search all of your resources at one time. The model shown in Figure 12.11 illustrates why discovery searching is faster and more efficient.

Figure 12.11. Web-Scale Discovery Search Model

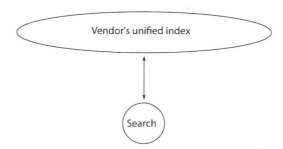

Web-scale discovery systems are also called discovery layers and discovery search. Like federated search, discovery search provides one search box to search all your databases and your catalog. Your library's special collections can even be added into the index and kept private for your own searching or shared with all the other libraries on that vendor's system. The major difference is the unified index.

The vendor takes the indexing information from every database it can, including your library catalog and special collections, and it puts all this information in one large index, the unified index. The system resides in the cloud. The vendor's servers host the index and the search software. A wider variety of searching is possible with a discovery search than a federated search, because the software no longer has to meet the lowest common denominator.

There are economies of scale for the vendor. Creating the unified index is a big expense, but adding libraries to the system is an easier task, and each of these libraries uses the same unified index. This creates more value for the vendor, leading to lower prices as its systems mature and gain clients.

For your library, a discovery search system should require less work on your part than a federated system. With more search feature and the ability to search everything in and owned by your library or all the libraries in your district, discovery search is being hailed as a revolution in libraries. In a webinar presented by SerialsSolutions, Dr. Michael Eisenberg, one of the creators of the Big6, said that teaching students how to search could be de-emphasized because of the effectiveness of discovery search (Eisenberg 2012).

Discovery search offers a Google-like search experience for your students, while providing Google-like access to *all* of your resources, increasing the value and usage of your resources. It provides a useful starting point and a familiar interface for students, while also providing many options for limiting and refining search results, and not requiring the knowledge of which databases to use for their information need.

Challenges still remain. We are not to the level of effectiveness that Eisenberg mentioned. Information overload is an increased problem as more results are returned. Confusion about what is being presented in the results list, how it is ranked, and how to find a known item, an item you know you own and can access, that did not show up at the top of the list is a major issue. Students still need to be taught how to use discovery search to get the best and most relevant materials from it or to find specific types of information, like your audiobook collection. One study compared college student search results on using two different discovery services, plus Google Scholar, and a standard library resource, and one of their conclusions was that a discovery search does not eliminate the need for information literacy instruction but may make instruction easier because it can focus on one interface (Asher, Duke, and Wilson 2013). Discovery search is still a young product, and it should continue to improve with time.

SEARCH WORKSHEET

Figure 12.12 shows a sample worksheet to aid in the construction of searches. It will help with the proper use of Boolean ANDs and ORs. It should help with the use of keywords and synonyms. It also mimics the advanced

Figure 12.12.   Search Worksheet

Search Statement Worksheet						
Research Question						
		Keyword	OR	Synonym 1	OR	Synonym 2
	1st concept					
AND	2nd concept					
AND	3rd concept					
AND	4th concept					
Search Statement						

search screens that you and your customers will see in various databases and builds familiarity with this important search option.

Each row represents one concept. As you work from left to right filling in synonyms, you add an OR between each term. When the search is executed, the first concept line is OR'ed together, then the terms on the second concept line are OR'ed together, then the third, and so on. Finally, each line is AND'ed to the other. You can add more columns for more synonyms or add more rows for more concepts, but the more you add, the more confusing the form and the search become.

Figure 12.13 shows an example of how to use the worksheet.

Figure 12.13.   Search Worksheet with Example

Search Statement Worksheet						
Research Question *What effect is genetically modified foods having on the health of insects and birds?*						
		Keyword	OR	Synonym 1	OR	Synonym 2
	1st concept	*gmo's*	OR	*"genetically modified foods"*		
AND	2nd concept	*insects*	OR	*birds*		
AND	3rd concept	*health*	OR	*illness*	OR	*death*
AND	4th concept					
Search Statement *(gmo's OR "genetically modified foods") AND (insects OR birds) AND (health OR illness OR death)*						

Vocabulary

and

Boolean operators

controlled vocabulary

database

discovery search

federated search

field

keyword

not

or

order of execution

phrase

record

relevance

retrieval

search engine

synonym

Venn diagram

Questions

Can you draw the parallels between an electronic database and print reference source or a novel?

Which operator(s) work best to narrow the focus of a search, and why?

Is it better to use truncation or the OR operator to find synonyms, and why?
How is discovery search different from using Google?

Assignment

Create a Venn diagram for the search statement shown in Figure 12.14.

Pick a vendor-supplied database and practice your searching. Pick one term from each column, search them separately, and then combine them using Boolean operators. Add a third term of your choosing and combine and recombine them until you feel you understand what the search is doing.

Use the blank search worksheet from Figure 12.12 and write a search statement for the following research question. "What effect does interacting with dogs and cats have on the health of elderly patients?" Run your search in a vendor-supplied database and record your results. Was this an effective search?

Figure 12.14. Practice Search Terms

Column 1	Column 2
Birds	Environment
Elephants	Global warming
Frogs	Migration
Rabbits	Pollution
Whales	Predators

Chapter **13**

Search Specifics for Catalogs, Databases, and the Web

This chapter will discuss specific search functions available when searching library catalogs, commercial databases, and the Web. The chapter starts with a brief history of the library catalog that parallels the growth and development of library resources leading to the most amazing resource, the Web.

A VERY BRIEF HISTORY OF THE LIBRARY CATALOG

The library catalog has changed dramatically throughout its history. In its most current incarnation, the library catalog is the gateway to every resource the library owns or has access to in any format. The library catalog has a long history of evolutions and revolutions. This section outlines this development.

The *Merriam-Webster Online Dictionary* defines a "catalog" as "a complete enumeration of items arranged systematically with descriptive details" (Merriam-Webster, Inc. 2013d). That is an apt description of library catalogs regardless of their form. We will begin with the catalog's first form, the book catalog.

Book Catalogs

Book catalogs were the original catalogs. They were written out on scrolls or in books. There were even tablet catalogs dating from 2000 B.C. (Casson 2001). These first library catalogs were a response to growing collections that could no longer be managed from memory. The problem with book catalogs was in updating them. When new books were added to the collection, they were written into the margins or on pieces of paper that were stuck in the book until it became necessary to rewrite the whole book.

Book catalogs did not offer many points of access, but multiple copies could be made and shared with other libraries. This is how library holdings were shared not too long ago. The *National Union Catalog* was a publication of the Library of Congress. It included all of its library's holdings plus three-letter codes of other libraries, usually large university and public libraries that also owned the material. The *National Union Catalog* was published in the late 1970s and was very important to researchers and to the resource-sharing efforts of libraries. It was the best tool libraries had for a long time, but it was a large, expensive, multivolume set that was most likely owned only by large libraries.

Card Catalogs

Card catalogs were developed in the late 1800s (Chan 1994). The first cards were handwritten, and a particular style came to be used, which was later called "library script." The card catalog was a vast improvement over book catalogs. New materials could be added without the need to update the whole catalog. Most important, the card catalog easily allowed for multiple access points for finding materials. Each book typically had a card under the author's name, title of the book, and the subjects of the book. Each book had a minimum of three cards.

There were two types of card catalogs: dictionary catalogs that interfiled author's names with titles and subjects, and divided catalogs that separated the cards by type. Card catalogs were quite large, occupying tremendous floor space. Multiple customers could use the card catalog at the same time, but sharing your holdings with another library was not a possibility. Book catalogs continued to serve that role for a while. Both card and book catalogs allowed for serendipity. As you browsed for an item, you could easily find many other items that may pique your interest. Finally, card catalogs required a lot of maintenance to keep them up to date with all the material being added and withdrawn from the collection.

Computer Output Microfilm Catalogs

Computer output microfilm catalogs (COM cats) were an intermediate step and short lived. They were in many respects neither as nice as the card catalogs they replaced nor as nice as the computer catalogs that followed. COM cats came into their own in the early 1970s (Zink 1977) and were preceded by improvements in computers and another important library development, the MARC format. MARC stands for "machine readable cataloging." Using the MARC format, catalogers entered records into the computer. The computer could then manipulate the records to create all the author, title, and subject entries for a catalog and then output the catalog to microfilm (Chan 1994).

Multiple copies of COM cats could be distributed on microfilm or microfiche. This distribution was important for large library systems as it facilitated sharing resources. Consortiums of academic and state libraries used micro-fiche to create union catalogs, a catalog that listed the resources of all libraries in the consortium, that broadened access to their collections. COM cats were not economical for small and medium-sized libraries. The card catalog continued to serve the needs of those libraries.

Online Public Access Catalogs

Online public access catalogs (OPACs) were a revolutionary step forward for the library catalog and information retrieval. Search software was applied to the MARC record database of library holdings instead of printing a COM cat. We have discussed at length how electronic database searching works in Chapter 12. It was a significant improvement in efficiency and effectiveness over using any previous catalog. The cost of computers was coming down, which helped to make this system feasible. You could also have multiple terminals hooked up to your mainframe to allow multiple people to use the catalog at once.

Web Catalogs

OPACs evolved into the Web catalogs (WebPACs), or Web-based public access catalogs, we use today. To a searcher, there was a little difference between OPACs and WebPACs. They looked the same and did the same things. Initially, WebPACs were inferior to OPACs because the technology was new. They offered basic search features, but not the more advanced and powerful features that OPACs had, but that changed.

The big difference between the two was that WebPACs made sharing your resources with other libraries and customers easy. Anyone anywhere in the world with a computer, an Internet connection, and a Web browser can search your collections. Since they are Web based, WebPACs also allow for direct linking to electronic resources.

Open-Source Catalogs

Open source is an important, recent development in integrated library systems (ILSs) and their catalogs. Open-source software is freely available and can be modified by anyone, that is, anyone with the skills to do so. Examples of prominent and successful open-source software are the Linux operating system (http://www.linux.org), the Firefox Web browser (http://www.mozilla.org), and the productivity software suite LibreOffice (http://www.libreoffic.org).

Open source offers a number of advantages. There is no cost for the software, and no maintenance fees need to be paid to the vendor. The software cost and maintenance fees can be high for vendor-supplied library systems. There is a community of other users who supply support, fixes, and extensions to the open-source software for free. The disadvantage is that a skilled computer person is needed to set up and maintain the software. Depending on the complexity of the software and its deployment, this could be a part-time job for one person at a small library or a full-time job for multiple people at a large library or consortium.

Koha (http://www.koha.org) and Evergreen (http://evergreen-ils.org/) are two open-source library systems. The Wikipedia article on ILSs contains a list of open-source library systems (http://en.wikipedia.org/wiki/Integrated _library_system; "Integrated Library System" 2013). Koha was originally designed with smaller libraries in mind and is used by many school libraries and school districts. Evergreen was designed for large libraries and consortia. These systems offer all of the features of their proprietary, vendor-supplied counterparts. If you do not have a person to install and maintain your open-source system, there are companies willing to provide those services and hosting services as well for a price.

THE LIBRARY CATALOG

Your library catalog is the window into the library. You should be able to find everything the library owns and has access to through it. Everything you own and purchased access to should be listed in the library catalog, all of your books, media, and electronic resources, and there should be links to those electronic resources that make locating them seamless.

Searching Catalogs

Library catalogs share many common search features, such as keyword, field, basic, and advanced searching. In addition, browse searching is often an option that allows you to get close enough to what you are after and then move up and down through a list arranged alphabetically by title or author or arranged by call number. To see and search a variety of library catalogs, visit LibWeb (http://www.lib-web.org/), which lists catalogs from public and academic libraries around the world.

Default Search

The default search in library catalogs is a keyword search that searches the author, title, subject, and perhaps additional fields like series. This search usually works well for most of your students' information needs. This is the broadest search you can do, and it will retrieve the most records, but it is not the most efficient search. With high retrieval comes low relevance. However, this problem is often mitigated by the fact that your catalog has the smallest database of any of your electronic database resources. Boolean operators and the phrase operator along with truncation are implemented in catalog search engines.

Field Search

Field searching is one way to improve the efficiency and accuracy of a catalog search. Field searching is often accessed from the advanced search screen and presents the customer with multiple search boxes and field options for each search box. If you are looking for books by a specific author, then use the author search function that limits your search to the author field. This is an important option to ensure you find items written by the author and not items about the author. Alternatively, a search that is limited to the subject field is the best way to find resources about an author, for example, Poe, as opposed to works written by him.

Subject searching is the way to ensure you find all items about a specific topic. Catalogs use *Library of Congress Subject Headings.* Most people will not know the official subject terms for their subjects. A well-worded default search is often the better option. However, it is a good idea to examine the records for some of the items retrieved through the default keyword search and see what subject headings are being used. Then, if necessary, the search can be modified or a new search can be done using the official term.

If you know the title of an item or a few words from the title, then a title search is the effective option. Problems arise with title searching when you think you know the title. Searching the wrong title can easily give you a false zero. The item is really in your collection, but you failed to find it.

Advanced search allows you to combine a title search with an author search, even if it is one word from the title and the author's first name. This helps reduce the problem of not knowing all of the specific information you need for an author or title search alone. Advanced search allows you to construct complex searches for information or search fields that may not be available in the default search, like journal title or ISBN number.

Limiting Searches

Catalogs provide a means to limit your search results by specific characteristics. Database vendors call this a faceted search. For example, you can often limit your results by the type of material, language, and location. This feature allows your search for dinosaurs to be limited to DVDs in Spanish or print resources in your reference collection.

Vendors

There are many vendors of ILSs. To find ILS vendors, go to Library Technology Guides (http://www.librarytechnology.org/companies.pl; Breeding 2011). You can search for a specific ILS company or select a vendor from the list. You will get basic contact information, including its Web site, but, more important, you can get a list of the libraries using this vendor's ILS. This is a great way to sample many different catalogs in a short period of time. If you prefer, you can go to the library search page of the same site and find out which ILS is used by your favorite libraries.

No library can function without a catalog. It is essential. It is a powerful tool that you need to be familiar with in order to provide the best service to all your customers.

COMMERCIAL DATABASES

Vendor-supplied database search engines can make use of Boolean, phrase, and proximity operators. They support truncations and often wildcard searching.

Default Search

The default search is a keyword search that searches most of the fields in the database. The major exception is the full text. In most databases, you must specify in the advanced search screen that you want to search the full text even though the database contains full-text information. There are exceptions. Westlaw (http://www.westlaw.com) and LexisNexis (http://www.lexisnexis .com) default to a full-text search.

The default search is a single search box with few or no options designed to simplify searching and presents a familiar Google look to the search.

Advanced Search

While a Google-like search box may be familiar to your customers, it is not the best way to learn how to search effectively. The search worksheet from Chapter 12 is similar to the advanced search screens from vendor-supplied databases. It is also an easier way to learn how Boolean operators work and interact with search terms in both simple and complex searches. While many databases show three rows of search boxes, additional rows can be added.

Fields are accessible from the advanced search screen. Fields can be combined and searched in any way that best works for the search. For example, you can search for all of the articles written by a specific author that appeared in a specific journal.

Faceted Search

Faceted search allows you to refine your search by limiting it to specific kinds of information. According to *Webster's*, a facet is "any of the definable aspects that make up a subject ... or an object" (Merriam-Webster, Inc. 2013e). The number and type of facets available depends on the database being searched. One common facet to limit your results is a year or range of years that the items need to be published within. Other facets limit the type of resource to scholarly journals, popular magazines, or trade publications. Facets can limit search results to books, eBooks, audiobooks, or videos. Facets are easy to apply; checking a box is all that is required. Most facets are applied after an initial search, but some can be applied before searching begins. Facets provide a means to focus the search results without applying additional terms to the search. Some facets will prove to be more useful than others depending on the information need.

THE WEB

The Web is massive. To find information from such a huge entity takes a special kind of search engine and an incredibly large index. Google indexes 60 trillion Web pages ("How Search Works: The Story" 2013). That is astounding! Anyone can create a Web page on any topic. The Web is not structured like a database, and every "record" or Web page contains full text. These factors make searching the Web a potentially difficult proposition. Retrieval will be very high, so we will anticipate very low relevance.

Search Engines

There is more than one way to search the Internet, and Bing is not the only other way. There are many Web search engines available. To find them, you can google it. Of course, there is also an excellent list of search engines in Wikipedia ("List of Search Engines" 2013). Google is the best-known search engine in the world and is either the second ("2013 BrandZ Top 100" 2013) or fourth ("Best Global Brands 2012" 2013) most valuable brand in the world depending on which brand consultants' reports you read.

Bing and Google use Web crawlers to find Web pages and add them to their indexes. Web pages do not have defined fields, so the crawlers have to make note of where words are found in the documents they index. This feature helps with relevancy ranking, the method these indexing services use to present the results that they find. The algorithms used by Web search engines to create their list of relevancy-ranked results are not the same. They are proprietary information that differentiates the results received by one search engine from another.

A search in both Google and Bing for the five words "South American frogs global warming" retrieves one common result in the top 10 hits. You can use a site like SearchBoth.com (http://us.searchboth.net) that will use two search engines for your search and display the results side by side. This search illustrates the differences in the relevancy-ranking algorithms.

Relevancy ranking is extremely important to Web search engines because of the vast amounts of information available. For example, the five-term search given in the previous paragraph produced more than 2.2 million results on Google and more than 6.5 million on Bing. This answers the question of why students do not browse past the first page! The theory behind relevancy ranking is that the sources that best fit your search criteria and that you most likely want to use will rise to the top of the very large list of results. Your search terms will be found in the title of the Web page and the headers used in the Web page and will show up many times in the text. The sites at the top of the list will also be linked to by other Web sites more frequently than those lower on the list.

Relevancy ranking is a method to address the issue of relevance versus retrieval that we examined in Chapter 12. By sorting results in a ranked order from best to worst based on a formula, relevancy ranking will move false hits to the bottom of the list of results and present the best results from large quantities of information. However, clever Web page designers know the methods that will increase the rank of their Web pages in search results. This contributes to false hits, or at the very least, to push the more relevant hits further down the list where they may not be used.

Visible and Invisible Web

It is important to remember that Web search engines do not search the whole Web. New sites may take days or weeks to be found by Web crawlers. More important, Web search engines do not search the invisible Web. The visible Web is that portion of the Web that is accessible to all. No logins or passwords are necessary to search the visible Web. The invisible Web is sources you purchase for your library. These sources either require a login and password or are restricted by an IP address. These resources are invisible to Web search engines.

Web Search

When Web search engines first appeared, they used an implied OR between the words in a search statement. They had to rely on relevancy ranking to bring the best results to the top. When Google appeared, it used an implied AND between words in a search statement, and it achieved higher relevancy than its competitors, which enabled it to dominate the market.

Besides supporting an implied AND, Web search engines support the double quotation marks as the phrase operator. The minus sign, –, is the Web search equivalent of the NOT operator. When placed directly in front of the word you do not wish to find, for example, –economic, the minus sign will exclude that term from the search results. Truncation is not necessary with Web search, as the search engines are advanced enough to consider various forms of the keywords being searched.

A new development in Web search engines is the provision of answers in addition to a list of resources. You can use the search box as a calculator and not just for simple addition. A search for "square root of 4" yields the answer 2. A search for "5 euros in U.S. dollars" brings up the answer based on today's exchange rate. A search for the early twentieth-century American author James Branch Cabell results in his photo, a brief overview, and his birth and death dates. Not all of these types of searches work, yet. A search for "calories in an apple" pulls up the answer in Google, but not in Bing at the moment. You still receive a list of results for these searches, but the answer is provided at the top of the list or at the right-hand side of the list. This obvious evolution of the search engine makes it an even more valuable resource for students and librarians.

A simple search for "movies" pulls up a list of films playing near you, with show times, reviews, and trailers. This is amazing and is brought to you by search engines that tract your personal information. They know where you are and what you search for. They have built a profile of who you are based on your behavior online, favorite sites, and favorite searches. This feature leads to a problem that should concern all users of Web search engines. The results you receive from a search on your personal computer or based on your login identification are unique to you. Two people searching for the same information about the federal government will receive different results because one has visited left leaning sites, while the other has visited right leaning sites (Blakeman 2010; "Search Engine Update" 2012). The results received are not the best results based on relevancy-ranking algorithms, but are the best sites for the searcher based on his or her past behavior online. In other words, you are frequently getting information that supports your current beliefs, as opposed to the best information available that might challenge your beliefs. These types of search results are not conducive to learning, growth, or broadened perspectives, but only serve to reinforce existing beliefs that may not be based on fact. This is the dark side of Web search engines of which few are even aware (Pariser 2011).

Advanced Web Search

Google offers an advanced search screen, but Bing removed this feature. However, the advanced search screen in Google is available post search only. After your initial search is executed, you gain access to the advanced search option, which is a link at the bottom of the screen. From the advanced search screen, you can specify the type of media you want to find, like pictures, videos, PowerPoint slides, or Excel spreadsheets. You can limit your search to specific domains like .edu, .com, or .gov. You can specify terms that have to be included in your results, AND; terms that may be present, OR; terms to exclude, NOT; and the exact phrases that need to be matched.

Both Bing and Google offer faceted search. You can apply any number of limiting facets to your search results, including the date of publication. An image search can be limited by the size of the images. Video searches can be limited by the length and resolution of the video.

Semantic Search

Semantic search is also called the natural language search. Ask Jeeves differentiated itself from the competition by encouraging customers to type a question in the search box. Ask Jeeves parses the question and provides answers from its database of answers. A standard search engine provided additional results. Ask Jeeves was the illusion of natural language searching. Employees associate specific questions with concepts, and then the search displays the information gathered by those employees as the first results (Sullivan 1998). This was a labor-intensive and expensive approach, further limited by the size of the database that the employees could create and maintain. With Web search engines improving constantly and the number of Web sites increasing, this model was not sustainable.

Semantic search tries to understand the meaning of the words in the search statement and does not merely execute a search based on the keywords entered. Here are two questions:

What killed the dinosaurs?

What caused the dinosaurs to become extinct?

The answer to both of these questions is the same. A semantic search should recognize that these two questions share the same meaning. This is a very difficult task for a search engine, because languages are so complex with multiple synonyms, various sentence structures, and contextual meanings. Searching each of these questions in Google returned only one common result from the first 10 results. The common item used both the keywords "killed" and "extinction." Web search engines are working toward this broader understanding of language and incorporate advances as they are made, but semantic search is not effective, yet.

Hakia (http://www.hakia.com) and Lexxe (http://www.lexxe.com) are semantic search engines. They believe that their products will result in better searches than traditional Web search engines, but interpreting the meaning of the question is difficult for them. A search in both Hakia and Lexxe for the questions mentioned earlier produced two very different result sets in both search engines just as they did in Google. While semantic search engines have gotten better, these results reinforce the importance of the keywords you choose to search.

Hierarchical Search

A hierarchical search organizes information into categories by subject just like folders of information on your computer. It is an attempt to impose order on the Web. Hierarchical search allows you to browse through the categories and subcategories of information, narrowing the focus of your search until you find what you want. The hierarchical arrangement is also called a directory.

Yahoo (http://www.yahoo.com) started with hierarchical search and was the most famous purveyor of this approach. Items in each subject category were selected by editors at Yahoo and not found by Web crawlers. This was a basic quality check. Searching at Yahoo resulted in searching through these directories for results, and not the Web as a whole. Yahoo no longer has a link to its directories on its home page. You need to go directly to Yahoo! Directory (http://dir.yahoo.com) or search it to find the link.

This type of searching is no longer popular for the Web at large. It suffers from the same problems that plagued Ask Jeeves. There are specialty hierarchies available like the Internet Public Library (http://www.ipl.org), which lists selected resources in various subject areas. The site is hosted by Drexel University and maintained by students and volunteers ("About Ipl2" 2012).

Subject Search Engines

There are specialized Web search engines that limit themselves to a particular subject. USA.gov (http://www.usa.gov) is the U.S. government's portal to all the information it produces, plus information from state, county, and city governments. It has a search engine to find all the information available and a directory structure to drill down through to find information on a topic.

Metasearch

A metasearch engine is a search engine that searches other search engines. It is the Web equivalent of federated search. A search submitted to a metasearch engine is in turn submitted to multiple Web search engines. The results are displayed either in a combined list or by listing results from each search engine used. Dogpile (http://www.dogpile.com) is an example of a metasearch engine. It searches Google, Yahoo, and Yandex (http://www.yandex.com), which is a major eastern European Web search engine.

The advantages of a metasearch engine are the same as those for federated and discovery search. Multiple sources are searched at once, and retrieval is high. The results look like standard Web search engine results, and it is easy to miss where the results come from. The first few pages of results on Dogpile come from Yahoo search. So unless the results are browsed deeply, you may be better served using a standard Web search engine.

Clustering search engines take the metasearch engine one step farther. Results are combined and ranked, then categorized by subject matter, and put into groups or clusters that can be accessed from the results page. The clusters show you a more specific breakdown of your topic and allow you to choose a group of similar results without the need to browse through pages of results to find them. Yippy (http://yippy.com) is a good example of a clustering search engine. A search of Yippy for "dinosaur extinction" resulted in a list of about 100 top results from the metasearch and many subject clouds as the clusters are called such as "Evolution," "Million years ago," "Mysterious," "Paleontology, Research," and "Impact of an Enormous Meteorite." You can also see how the items cluster by the source of origin and by domain. The subject clusters are a great feature that helps customers see the types and emphasis of the materials they have retrieved.

With metasearch, you need to be aware of the resources that are being used to find the search results. A metasearch may use a number of search engines, but if it does not use one of the big search engines or displays pages of results from only one of the search engines, how good will the results be?

Kid-Friendly Search Engines

There are search engines designed for student use that provide safe searching. These search engines prevent inappropriate sites from showing up on the list of results. KidRex (http://www.kidrex.org) uses Google safe search to provide its results. It has a colorful, fun home page with Google search box. The list of results looks much like the standard Google results list. KidzSearch.com (http://www.kidzsearch.com) is another Google-powered safe search engine. Both of these search engines work in the very familiar Google manner. Boolify (http://www.boolify.org/), as in George Boole, uses a unique drag-and-drop interface to help students build a Google safe search. As students build a search, they can see the Google search statement they are creating as it will be executed and can learn how to create advanced Google searches. Bing is currently piloting a program called Bing for Schools (http://www.bing.com/schools) that brings safe Bing searches to the whole school. KidsClick! (http://www.kidsclick.org) searches a listing of good and appropriate sites for children that are selected and maintained by librarians. You can also browse the site by Dewey Decimal range or alphabetically.

A Web search is the first place many people turn to for an information need. A Web search engine is most likely to be the first search engine a student uses and their introduction to searching an electronic resource. There are many problems with searching the Web. While it is easy to execute a search, it is not necessarily easy to do a good search. People tend to choose Web sites not on the quality of the content, but on how pretty the site is and whether they already agree with the content (Anderson 2008). While the Web is a truly amazing resource with the potential to answer many questions with quality information, by its very democratic nature, it is also a source of bad, misleading, and intentionally harmful information. The Web is the easiest-to-use and least-understood resource. For these reasons, you need to know this resource well in order to teach your students how to find good, factual, and informative sites, while teaching them how to spot the bad ones.

Searching is a vitally important skill for you to master. Knowing how search engines work and how to search electronic resources efficiently and effectively will not only make you a better librarian now but prepare you deal with the changes that the future will bring. The better you understand how search works across all of your resources, the better you will be able to teach search skills to your students and help them become information literate in this electronic age.

Vocabulary

advanced search	invisible Web
author search	metasearch
clustering	open-source software
default search	relevancy ranking
faceted search	semantic search
full-text searching	subject search
hierarchical search	union catalog
integrated library system	visible Web

Questions

Of all the developments in the library catalog, which one do you think is the most revolutionary, and why?

How do facets work, and how are they different from advanced search?

Does metasearch work better than a single search engine search in the real world? Explain why?

Assignment

Compare and contrast searching and the search results from KidsClick! and one of the Google-powered kids search sites. What are the advantages and disadvantages of each? Which returns better results? Which one will you use with your students, and why?

Chapter **14**

Assessment and Evaluation of Reference and Instruction

This chapter examines what assessment or evaluation is, how to do them, how to interpret them, and, most important, how to use the results.

WHAT IS ASSESSMENT?

Assessment, or evaluation, is the means of discovering the quality of library services and programs. It is the method to determine what students already know and what they have learned. It is the way to demonstrate the value of the library to stakeholders: principals, teachers, parents, and students. Assessment is essential to all libraries, and it is important to assess your reference skills, your reference collections, and your information literacy (IL) instruction to improve your services.

PLANNING FOR ASSESSMENT

Before you assess a program or evaluate a colleague's performance at the reference desk or instruct a class, you need to plan the what, why, and how of assessment. It is like building a lesson plan. You need to know what you want to do, how you are going to do it, how you will judge if you did it well, and what you will do with that information, but first you need to know why you are doing it at all. To answer "why," think about whether this information you gather in your assessment is going to be reported to the principal or made available to parents.

What is the ultimate goal or purpose of the assessment? If you are evaluating your staff's performance at the reference desk, then the goal would be to improve reference service by identifying strengths and develop programs or trainings to address any weakness that is discovered. Will the results of this assessment be used in performance evaluations and reported to the principal, or is the assessment designed to be informal and used in-house only for the purpose of gauging staff knowledge and training needs?

With the "what" and "why" answered, you need to consider how you will conduct the assessment. We will examine the types of assessments more thoroughly later. The first consideration is, what yardstick will you use to measure success? If you are evaluating your staff at the reference desk, you could use your own reference service policy if you have one, or you could use the *Guidelines for Behavioral Performance of Reference and Information Service Providers* to give you a yardstick to measure performance. You inform your staff about the assessment and give them copies of the guidelines so they know what you will be doing.

Next, you decide how to use the guidelines in the assessment process. You develop a form and score each transaction on a scale of one to five in each of the areas covered by the guidelines. You record the questions received and the answers given if time permits. Figure 14.1 is an example of an evaluation form that you may want to modify or use. You evaluate all members of the staff by observing them as they answer questions from students, as opposed to assigning one person to evaluate another or everyone taking a turn evaluating everyone else.

Now, you compile all the information gathered and generate an average score and individual scores. Finally, you evaluate the assessment to discover what you learned. With an average score of 4.5 out of 5, you are very happy with how everyone performed, but there were a number of times that no answer was provided. You examine the questions to determine why they could not be answered. If you find that the questions are impossible or difficult to answer, then you know that resources are needed in these areas. If you find that the questions could have been answered quickly from the resources you own, then you know that staff members need training to become aware of these resources and on how to use them.

Through this assessment process, you learned that your staff members are attentive, polite, and professional and try hard to provide excellent service to your students. You have also learned that they need greater awareness of the resources you have. You need to take action on what you learned through the assessment process. You implement a training plan to introduce new and old resources alike to your staff during the first 10 minutes of the weekly staff meeting to raise an awareness of the library's resources. Lastly, you follow up six months later with a short assessment that checks staff awareness of library resources, and you find that resource introductions at staff meetings have improved staff knowledge. This is the assessment process. It takes time, planning, and follow-through to do well and achieve the goal of improving library services.

Figure 14.1. Reference Evaluation Forms

Name: Date: Time: Place:

	1 Worse	2	3	4	5 Better
Approachability					
Interest					
Listening/inquiring					
Searching skills					
Follow-up					

Comments about behavioral performance:

Questions from users:

_____

_____

_____

_____

_____

_____

_____

_____

_____

_____

_____

_____

_____

_____

_____

_____

TYPES OF ASSESSMENT

We will examine three types of assessment in the following sections: quantitative, summative, and formative. Each type of assessment has its own strengths and weaknesses. Alone, none of these types of assessment can fully describe your library or the services you provide. Used in combination, a more meaningful picture of your library will emerge through assessment.

Quantitative Assessments—Statistics

Statistics are part of the assessment process. They represent a quantitative measure of how much was spent, how much was done, and how many were taught for example. There are two types of statistics in your library. Input measures represent the resources allocated to the library at the start of the fiscal year. This is the library budget and its breakdown for expenditures on staffing and materials. Input measures are also starting points. How many items are in the collection at the start of the year, and how many computers and tablets you have in the library?

Output measures are the consequences of the inputs into the system. It is what your budget buys. Gate count is an output measure because it is the result of hours of operation, which in turn relates to staffing. The number of items added to the collection and the number of items circulated are typical statistics collected by libraries, and they are measures of output.

Gathering these types of statistics is generally easy. Your integrated library system should be able to provide you with all the circulation statistics you will need. You will need to think about the other statistics you want to gather and how you want to gather them. For example, you should collect statistics on how many reference questions you answer. You may even want to break down your reference statistics by the number you received at the desk in person and the number you received through your chat service, or you may want to track how many questions deal with the social science, the humanities, and the sciences so you know which teachers' students are using the library the most. The more categories you have, the harder it is to collect statistics. Decide which statistics are important to collect; then after a year, determine whether they really are important to collect.

You should also collect the number of IL instruction sessions you conducted and the number of students present for each one. You can combine this information with your lesson plans and determine how many of your students received instruction and in which standards.

Spreadsheets and databases are two good ways to keep track of statistics. They have the added benefit of making it easy to work with the data and produce reports. You can create forms that enable you to collect statistics in real time as you answer questions at the reference desk. You can also easily compare one year to another and create charts that show the changes from year to year.

Interpreting Statistics   Statistics need to be interpreted to have meaning. A year's worth of statistics means nothing if there is no point of reference. You could give your principal a report that says you circulated 5,000 books, answered 200 reference questions, and did 15 instruction sessions for a total of 300 students. These numbers may indicate that you were busy, but they say nothing else. They are data. They need a context to begin to tell a story. If you mentioned in your report that each of these figures is up 5 percent from the previous year or if you mentioned that your numbers are 10 percent lower than other schools in the district or 10 percent higher, then you have a story to tell. You have a means of interpreting the statistics so that they make some sense. This is data analysis.

"Figures lie, and liars figure" is an old saying about how easy it is to misinterpret statistics unintentionally or deliberately. As an example, you discover that 50 percent of all overdue material was checked out to seniors at your high school. This is a disproportionate number. Common sense says that it should be 25 percent at the most. You report this statistic to your principal, and you inform her that you will implement a program to bring this number down.

There could be many factors influencing that number. Fifty percent of your library users could be seniors, or 50 percent of all your circulations could be to seniors. The high figure could be the result of one or two seniors who checked out an inordinate amount of materials and were late returning all of them. Perhaps there is no other factor influencing the number, but the percentage of loans that result in overdue materials is less than 1 percent, making seniors responsible for less than 0.5 percent of loans that result in overdues. Is that a real problem that needs to be addressed?

In another example, you have seen a 5 percent increase in circulation of materials in each of the past two years, but your enrollment has remained flat. This is good news, and you want to get the word out that your stewardship of the library has resulted in greater use of resources. How do you explain the increase and confirm that your hard work has paid off? You have already ruled out enrollment increases as a possible contributing factor. Your library hours have not changed in that time, and your budget increases were enough only to offset inflation, so these factors should be unrelated to the increase. When you examine your statistics, you see that you did more collaborative instruction with teachers in each of those years, and your gate count went up. The gate count could be partially responsible for the increase in circulation, and the increased instruction could be responsible for the gate count and circulation increases. In other words, your actions did result in an increase in library circulations.

These examples should illustrate the importance of keeping statistics. Having multiple years' worth of statistics allows you to track changes and chart progress. It gives you the means you need to interpret the statistical data you are collecting. No matter how many statistics you collect nor how well you interpret them, they do not speak to quality.

Summative Assessments

A summative assessment is a measure of quality. A summative assessment is the grade given to a student on a test or at the end of a term. It is a measure of learning. It is a teaching evaluation. It is a common and a familiar form of assessment.

There are a number of ways that a summative assessment can be used in the library. The evaluation of staff performance in answering reference questions as mentioned earlier is an example of a summative evaluation. You are grading the performance of your staff over a given period of time.

One way to use a summative evaluation with students is to give a short pre-test at the beginning of an instruction session. At the end of the instruction session, you give a short posttest. Given the information you collected, you can measure student learning from your instruction session as you compare the pretest results with the posttest test results. You can ask the teacher of the class you are doing the instruction for to give your teaching a score based on how well you met the goals enumerated in the lesson plan and how well you imparted the information. This feedback could be invaluable in improving your teaching.

Formative Assessments

A formative assessment is designed to improve teaching. It is a quick assessment to determine what students already know or do not know, and their responses are used to change the course of their instruction to fit their needs. It is not formal, nor is it graded. It is a way to monitor student progress, and it should be done often and kept simple.

You can start an instruction session by asking students to take a minute to write down what they know about using the library catalog. As you sort quickly through the answers, you make mental notes of the responses and see what your students already know, what they do not know, and what they have wrong. If your students seem to know how to conduct a basic search but do not know where to find the call number on the record or how to find the book on the shelf, then make an adjustment to your instruction to spend time going over these issues.

There are many kinds of formative assessments like journaling, reflection papers, peer reviews, self-assessments, and discussions. There are many resources that will help you pick and use a formative assessment. As an example, the Illinois State Board of Education has put together a list of formative assessments (http://www.isbe.net/common_core/pdf/da-form-asmt-chart.pdf). It can be as simple as asking students if they understood what you just explained and using a different example if necessary to illustrate your point. Formative assessments should be done every time you do an instruction session or answer a reference question. Asking a student if the answer you gave answered his or her question or if the student understood how you searched that database is a formative assessment. Formative assessments are an important tool for learning how well you are doing and what your students need.

SURVEYS

Surveys may be used for either summative or formative assessments. A survey can solicit self-assessments, opinions, and knowledge of facts. A single survey can ask students to write one sentence about what they learned during an instruction session, test their learning with a couple true/false and multiple-choice questions, and ask them if they found the information presented useful. This survey could be completed in a minute at the end of an instruction session that is presented in a computer lab.

Most surveys you administer should be anonymous, which allows the respondents to express freely their opinions without the fear of repercussions, and students should know that the survey is anonymous for that reason. There are instances where you will not be able to offer anonymity. For example, if you ask a teacher to evaluate an instruction session, it cannot be anonymous. However, remember your professionalism, and take any criticism as suggestions to improve your teaching and not as a personal attack.

Surveys may be quickly and easily generated in free services like Survey-Monkey (https://www.surveymonkey.com). The free plan allows for surveys of no more than 10 questions, with no more than 100 responses. That should be enough to get feedback from an instruction session.

Another alternative is to use Google Forms, a part of Google Drive. You can create a form with multiple types of questions. The form can be e-mailed to a group of people, or you can link to the form with the supplied Web address. The results are stored in a Google Drive spreadsheet, so you can examine, extract, and interpret the results. Surveys offer an efficient means to collect information about library services from various stakeholders and should be part of your assessment program.

EVALUATING REFERENCE SERVICE

You can take three approaches to assessing reference services. You can assess the quality of the staff providing reference service, or you can assess customer satisfaction with the service they received from the staff. Finally, you can combine the first two approaches to develop a more complete picture of how well the service is functioning. You may choose to evaluate your staff in fall and assess customer satisfaction in spring. When you evaluate is not important. What matters is that you evaluate in a conscientious and professional manner.

REFERENCE EVALUATION

There are a few approaches to evaluating staff engaged in reference work. You can conduct an unobtrusive study, or you can observe the staff while they are working. In an unobtrusive study, you recruit customers to ask a set of preselected questions of your staff without them knowing what the questions will be. You do want to tell your staff what you are doing, and give them some general dates. You do not want the evaluation to be a surprise, and you do not want to make your staff feel spied upon with the intent of punishing them for any mistakes they might make.

In a study from 2002 of e-mail and chat reference services from public and academic libraries, it was seen that these services achieved only a 55 percent success rate in answering questions, which is the same number that in-person reference studies often found (Kaske and Arnold 2002). These studies lead to the mythical 55% Rule, that librarians supply the right answer only slightly more than half of the time. Like many of these studies, this study had to judge what a correct answer and what an incorrect answer would be. The questions in the study were supposed to be representative of typical questions. Most of the questions in this particular study were difficult to answer.

For example, one of the questions asked is, where and from what Chaucer died. The first part of this question is easy to answer. Reference sources frequently list when and where people died, like *Almanac of Famous People*. Finding Chaucer's cause of death is beyond most reference resources, especially because the cause of death is not known. If you used this question in an unobtrusive evaluation of your staff and a staff member got the first part of the question correct but could not answer the second part, how would you score that transaction, as a success or a failure?

This is an issue with an unobtrusive study. How do you pick good, representative questions, and how do you score the answers to them? One approach is to use variations of questions you have received. Keep the questions straightforward, with resources in mind that may be used to answer them. Your students or teachers will be the ones asking the questions and recording responses, so make it easy for them.

Another consideration with the unobtrusive method of evaluation is, do you want the student who asks the question to also evaluate the staff member's performance on the behavioral guidelines? That may be asking too much of a student. Perhaps the student could record his or her feelings about the transaction. Was the librarian nice? Was the librarian helpful? If you do not have the student questioners do something like this, are you going to evaluate your staff's behavioral performance at all?

Unobtrusive evaluations work best in large environments with many employees and busy service desks. The questions and the customers remain anonymous. In a small library, the questions may stand out, and the unobtrusive evaluation becomes obvious. If there are only two of you, this method is obviously not going to work. In this case, the observational method discussed here would be a better choice.

The observational method is another means of conducting an evaluation of reference staff. It is also called a peer evaluation, because one peer is evaluating another. With this method, you perform the evaluation by sitting with your colleagues at the reference desk. You listen to the questions they receive and the answers they give, and you watch the behaviors they exhibit in helping students. This method is much easier to implement. There is no need to develop representative questions. There is no need to recruit and train students or teachers to participate in the process. There is no need to worry about how to evaluate behavior. You are the one doing it all.

A major concern with a peer evaluation is that your presence may have a major impact on the behavior of the person being evaluated. You are not experiencing the same behaviors that students experience from them when you are not there. You are seeing them on their best behavior, putting forth their best effort. As long as you are aware of this influence, this approach can be extremely valuable. Your presence may encourage greater awareness of how behaviors influence reference transaction in your staff and lead to improved behavior overall.

Another problem with this method that you will encounter as you shadow your colleagues is refraining from answering questions yourself. It is difficult to stand back, evaluate, and watch the transactions without offering help, especially if the desk gets busy. It is acceptable to answer a few questions or to intervene if the staff member is struggling with a question. You do want to make sure that your customers are getting appropriate answers, and you should have enough information to evaluate this transaction. You should try to direct the business to the person being evaluated to have enough transactions to make the evaluation meaningful.

When evaluating a colleague's reference transaction, examine his or her interaction with the questioner. Did the colleague discover what the customer was really asking? Then did the colleague choose an appropriate resource or database and good search terms? Expect that the colleague will use a different approach than you. We all think differently, and that is not what is being evaluated. Did the colleague arrive at the best answer your resources allow? Unfortunately, sometimes the correct answer is that you cannot answer that question at this time, and sometimes the correct answer is giving the customer a few resources, biographies of Chaucer, and telling him or her that he or she will have to look for the answer in these resources. With that in mind, judge the quality of the whole transaction with the *Guidelines for Behavioral Performance* in mind.

For any evaluation method, it is important to keep in mind what you are trying to do. You are trying to help students and teachers become more information literate. You are not always just trying to give them the right answer but to teach them to find right answers for themselves. Keep this idea in mind when designing a reference evaluation.

CUSTOMER SATISFACTION EVALUATION

Another method for evaluating reference service, library instruction, and library services in general is to survey the customers. This approach gathers your customers' perceptions about your services. Although these perceptions may not reflect the whole truth of what is going on in your library or even what happened with a specific transaction, they do represent the truth of your customers' experiences. Your teachers could perceive your library to be out of touch with the times. Perhaps this was the case a few years ago, but you have made a concerted effort to modernize and improve services; however, this erroneous negative perception is lingering and having a negative impact on your library. How you and the library are perceived by teachers, administrators, and students will impact your library programs. A survey is a good method to discover these perceptions.

You can have customers fill out a short survey immediately after a reference transaction. This can be a piece of paper that you hand them and ask them to drop in a box, or you can give them a slip of paper with a Web address on it where they can find the survey or point to a link on your library Web page. You can use the same approaches with a class following an instruction session and include the class teacher by having him or her fill out a different survey designed for teachers. These targeted surveys will help you improve your services and teaching. Keep the survey short and precise to collect more responses.

You can also do a much more general customer satisfaction survey of the library. This is not easy. First, the postservice surveys have a built-in clientele. You give the survey to the class you just instructed. In a general survey, you have to determine who you are going to survey. For example, if you survey only the students and teachers who come into your library, then you are not getting the opinions of the people who are not using your library and you cannot find out why they do not use the library.

You may give your survey to a random sample of students and teachers at your school instead of everyone. Although this may make the survey more manageable, it complicates the process because you have to determine how you will select the teachers and students you will survey. Do you want or need to collect demographic data in your survey? Will knowing the age, sex, and grade of your students affect the interpretation of the data? In other words, knowing how seniors feel about the library versus how freshman view the library may be an indicator of the success of your collaborations with teachers.

General customer satisfaction surveys require extensive planning. Determine what information you want to find out about your library and how you plan to use it. If you do not know how you will use the information from a question to improve your services, then the question is probably not worth asking. Decide who you want to survey and why. Enlist the cooperation of administration and find resources to help you. *Library User Survey Templates & How-Tos* (http://www.lrs.org/library-user-surveys-on-the-web) provides information on how to conduct a survey and three sample library surveys that will help you construct your surveys (Library Research Service 2013a).

It is a good idea to use services like SurveyMonkey and Google Forms over paper surveys, because they eliminate the need for data input and give you many options to manipulate the data. Keep your surveys short and precise. They are more likely to be answered. An alternative to a long customer satisfaction survey is to do multiple short surveys focused on one or two aspects of the library.

No matter how you decide to collect information from your customers, it is vitally important that you do so. The library is supposed to help its customers, and you need to know if the library is meeting that very fundamental goal. You need to take action on what you have learned and make necessary improvements, or the process is an empty one. If you discover a false negative perception of the library, then you know that you need to market all those great services you have to change that perception and give the library the standing it deserves.

SAMPLE EVALUATION FORMS

The sample forms in Figures 14.2 and 14.3 can be used as a posttransaction reference evaluation by students.

The form in Figure 14.2 is very simple and requires "yes" or "no" answers. Compiling the information from this survey would be very easy but not very granular. The example in Figure 14.3 uses a Likert scale to allow respondents to select a range of feelings about the question being asked. It also includes a

Figure 14.2. Simple Reference Transaction Evaluation

	Yes	No
Did the librarian help you find what you needed?	○	○
Was the librarian nice to you?	○	○

Figure 14.3. Reference Transaction Evaluation with Likert Scale

	Strongly Disagree	Disagree	Undecided	Agree	Strongly Agree
The answer I received was accurate and helpful.	○	○	○	○	○
The service I received from the librarian was respectful.	○	○	○	○	○
Comments					

comment box to allow the respondents to express an opinion. Compiling comments takes more time but can provide valuable information for improvement.

Next is a sample survey to be given to students following an instruction session (Figure 14.4). It has five questions. The first two use a Likert scale to evaluate the content and teaching of the session. The final three questions use a KWL (know, want to know, and learned) format to discover what students already know, what they expected to learn, and what they learned from the session. This information can give you a baseline and guide the changes you make to improve the instruction.

The example in Figure 14.5 is for the class teacher to give you feedback. The information solicited in this example should help you improve your sessions and teaching in the future.

WHAT IF IT IS ONLY YOU?

Although the concept of evaluation is an important one, some evaluations can be difficult if you are the only person in your library. How do you evaluate your performance at the reference desk?

Figure 14.4. Instruction Session Student Survey

	Strongly Disagree	Disagree	Undecided	Agree	Strongly Agree
The instruction I received should help me with my research.	○	○	○	○	○
The instructor did a good job explaining concepts.	○	○	○	○	○
List one thing that you already knew.					
List one thing that you wanted to learn.					
List one thing that you learned.					

Figure 14.5. Instruction Session Teacher Survey

	Strongly Disagree	Disagree	Undecided	Agree	Strongly Agree
The instruction met the needs of my class or assignment?	◯	◯	◯	◯	◯
The instructor did a good job explaining concepts.	◯	◯	◯	◯	◯
What other information needs to be part of this session?					
How could the instructor improve this session next time?					
What could the instructor do better?					

One method is to ask for help. It is best if you do not ask for help from the teachers and administrators in your school. They may be more than happy to help, but you would be better served by having a fellow librarian do the evaluation because of his or her knowledge of library collections, services, and work. Ask for help from colleagues at other schools first. If you cannot get the help you need, turn to the public library or academic library. Be sure you have planned what you want to do, so your colleagues know exactly what they are agreeing to do for you.

If you cannot find a colleague to help you, then try writing a short self-evaluation or an assessment of your experiences at the reference desk. This is a reflection paper like the ones we assign to our students. We can be overly critical of ourselves or overly generous. Reflecting on your performance should help you be fair and move away from the idea of criticizing performance and toward the idea of understanding performance and seeing opportunities for growth.

Another method you can try is to pick out one of the behaviors from the *Behavioral Performance Guidelines* and consciously think about that behavior while you are at the reference desk. For example, if you picked approachability, you need to be mindful of all of your behaviors that affect your approachability. Are you sitting with your arms crossed and slumped forward, or are you leaning far back in your chair with your arms dangling by your side, or are you sitting straight up looking out at the library? Do you bring work to the desk that you never look up from? Are you staring intensely at the computer monitor on your desk? Do you look up often from that work? Do you smile at everyone who walks into the library? Do you walk around the library? Do you ask students if you could help them? With practice, you will get better at seeing your behaviors and be able to identify your strengths and weaknesses. Concentrate only on one of the five guidelines at a time. Then next week, pick another behavior to develop.

Finally, you can also keep track of the questions you had trouble answering. When you get some free time, go back to these questions and try answering them again. However, take a different approach this time. Try different resources and different keywords, and use a new search strategy. After you look for the answer, evaluate your search strategy. If you found the answer this time, what did you do differently that worked and where did you go wrong the first time? If you still cannot find the answer, is there a resource missing from your collection that might have helped, can you get help from someone else, is there a good referral to an outside agency you could have given the student, or is there no good answer to the question?

REPORT WRITING

You completed a survey. You and your colleagues watched each other at the desk. You kept track of your reference transactions. You know how many instruction sessions you did and for how many students. You have collected a lot of information that took a lot of time and effort. What do you do with it? Write a report.

A report is a great way to get the word out about how well you are doing in the library and remind administrators of the important role the library plays in the successful education of students. Reports are useful because they force you to summarize and analyze the information you gathered. Your analysis of the information should guide your decision about library services and collections. A report also serves as institutional memory. It is your record of what you did in the past and how well it worked. By collecting information regularly, you will be able to spot patterns and identify trends while learning what you are doing well and what needs improvement.

You should write a report every year that summarizes the library's activities throughout the past year. Because you no doubt have to supply statistics to your principal and district, write your annual report at that time. Write reports about special projects at the time you complete the project so the information is fresh in your mind, and then include a summary of that report in your annual report. A report gives you a record of what happened, and each year, you can use the previous year's report as a template for your new report. Including statistics from previous years in your current report allows you to see and comment on trends. A report without analysis of the information presented is not worth doing, because it will not mean anything to the person who reads it. So always explain what your statistics are, what they mean, and what trends you may be able to see by looking at them.

Finally, evaluation is a learning experience. The more you evaluate, the easier it becomes, and the more you learn from the experience. You learn what your library is doing well and where you can improve. Evaluation results in an opportunity to improve your services and yourself. Writing a report allows you to record your experiences and share them with others. It preserves the knowledge you gained from the evaluation process and gives you insight into what to examine closely the next time. Evaluation should be an integral process within your library. Without the opportunity to assess, evaluate, and analyze what you are doing, you will not understand the successes or failures of your programs and services, and you will have missed an opportunity for growth.

THE VALUE OF YOUR LIBRARY

How do you measure the value of what you do? Can you put a price tag on your library's services? Collecting annual statistics is a part of the picture. Statistics can show the amount of use your library and specific services are receiving. Does that represent value? You can take your statistics and calculate cost per use, as we discussed in Chapter 7. Is that a better yardstick?

Cost per use does give you a good measure of value, but in a very limited way. How do we put a qualitative assessment on a quantitative price? Is a $5.00 cost per use simply too high, or are there other factors that need to be taken into consideration? What if that $5.00 represented the cost per reference question? What is your expert tutoring worth? What if the cost per reference question was $30.00 per question or more? Would you stop offering this service?

The Value of the Reference Collections

You can put a price on the books that are housed in your reference collection, but that figure will not represent the true scope of your reference collections. Your databases could be added into that figure, but your reference collections extend beyond those resources as well. Your whole library is your reference collection. *Any* resources you can access through any means are part of your reference collections, as are any referrals you make to outside agencies. Your knowledge and your skills are your reference collections. Although there is a price placed upon your service, your salary, it does not reflect your true worth to the students, teachers, administrators, and the school you serve.

We need to quantify some aspects of the reference collection to determine its use. Use is a measure of value. If your reference desk is busy and students use your print and electronic resources constantly, you can see and quantify some part of the value of the collection by counting its use.

The average age of your reference resources can affect their value and their use. If the average resource in your reference collection was published 10 years ago, the value of some specific resources will be low, because they are out of date. Older resources do not look inviting and fascinating. They look old and worn out. Updating your resources should help increase interest and use.

How well does the collection reflect the curriculum and student interests? A wonderful resource that no one uses is not a valuable resource. *The Oxford English Dictionary* is a wonderful resource but not for an elementary school library. Make sure your resources have appeal to both your teachers and your students.

Looking at use of collections does have a problem. The numbers mean nothing in a vacuum. You can compare your statistics to other libraries in your district. This would add a level of meaning to your numbers, but you need to be sure that you are comparing apples to apples. Comparing your statistics from this year to last year's statistics is a good way to show the success of marking campaigns, instruction sessions, and the appeal of new resources.

The Value of Instruction

It is difficult to calculate the value of your reference services. It is nearly impossible to place a value on your instruction services. How do you attach a figure to learning? We discussed the impact that IL instruction has on students in Chapter 10. We know that instruction improves search behaviors, choice of materials, and grades on assignments. A study in a college-level biology class found that students receiving IL instruction had more confidence in their library skills and had a more scholarly approach to research in addition to the benefits mentioned earlier (Ferrer-Vinent and Carello 2011). What is that worth to your school?

Although all of these improved individual skills are valuable in themselves, we need to examine the whole picture and determine whether the whole is bigger than the sum of its parts. What do these skills give to the students? If student research and work improve through instruction, what have the students gained? The easy answer is that students have learned IL skills. They are better users of information resources, and these benefits manifest in better course work.

If students conduct better research, select better databases and better resources, and do better work, then have they not also learned critical thinking skills as well as IL skills? This is the whole goal of IL skills, to create people who can fend for themselves and make informed decisions based on quality materials in an information-powered world. How can a value be placed on this?

The Value of the Library to the School

You can put a value on your library if you have this skill and background to conduct a return on investment (ROI) study, often called a cost-benefit analysis. ROI studies take into consideration direct benefits to the customers from library services and indirect benefits, mostly economic, that the community receives. The results of the study are stated as a ratio: for each dollar spent, the community receives X dollars in benefits. An ROI study of Florida's public libraries showed an ROI of $6.54 for every $1 spent (Monroe 2005). One study found that the average ROI for public libraries that have examined their value in this manner was between $4 and $6 (Matthews 2011). The author states that there is a place for the ROI number in library reporting, but that has not proven successful in preventing budget cuts or gaining budget increases, and there are no ROI studies of school libraries.

Using ROI may not work for school libraries at the moment. However, there are many other studies that show the value of the school library from a unique perspective that all stakeholders can understand. Many states have conducted studies of student achievement based on standardized test scores and analyzed factors that may have contributed to higher or lower scores. The American Association of School Librarians maintains a list of student achievement research reports (http://www.aasl.ala.org/essentiallinks/index.php?title=Student _Achievement) ("Student Achievement" 2013). The Library Research Services also maintains a list of the state studies (http://www.lrs.org/impact.php) and includes national studies, a nice infographic, and videos (Library Research Service 2013b). You can use this information to illustrate how libraries improve student achievement.

For example, a study in Kansas found that schools with full-time, certified school librarians generally outperformed those with part-time, noncertified librarians "across grades spans and subject areas" (Dow, Lakin, and Court 2012). A study of certified librarian staffing changes and reading scores in 2005 versus 2011 in Colorado found that schools that gained or had certified librarians had higher reading achievement and greater gains in reading scores than those that did not have or lost a certified librarian (Lance and Hofschire 2012). This study also found that schools with a full-time endorsed librarian outperformed schools with a half-time endorsed librarian.

A recent report summarized the findings of all of these state reports on value of libraries and endorsed or certified librarians to their schools (Kachel 2013). The report is broken down into sections that illuminate the findings that relate to staffing, collaboration, instruction, scheduling, access, technology, and so on. For example, in the collections section, you can find that schools with "well-resourced libraries" had higher writing scores and schools with newer collections or schools with higher circulations had higher test scores. In the budget section, you will find that larger library budgets are associated with higher achievement. Finally, in the collaboration section, one study showed that certified librarians who had clerical support staff helped their schools to get higher test scores than those without support staff. This document and the Web sites listed earlier will help you show stakeholders the tremendous value your library has in the education process.

Your Value

There are four areas in which you demonstrate your value to your school, administrators, teachers, students, and stakeholders. They are the library, technology, collaboration, and leadership. You want to create a library that is seen as welcoming, fair, equitable, and a place that provides great access to quality resources. You want your library to be viewed as a safe place for experiential learning and a place where everyone can get help from professionals who care about learning and teaching (Todd, Gordon, and Lu 2011).

You want your library to be viewed as a technology learning center where faculty and staff can receive hands-on training in a flexible and creative learning environment (Todd, Gordon, and Lu 2011). Use your reference skills to find and read articles from the professional literature, and explore training opportunities that will increase your awareness of new products, services, and trends. Try new software and evaluate it. Think about how you might be able to use it in the library and how your teachers might use it in the classroom. Then pass this information on.

You want your library to be seen as a collaborative environment where you and your staff want to work with teachers and administrators to improve student learning, support the curriculum, and provide IL instruction. Principals learn about the value of their libraries by working with their librarians, and they want to see you share your vision of the library, articulate goals for the library program, and work regularly with teachers (Shannon 2012).

You can achieve all of this when you lead. Leadership is having a vision and working to achieve it. It is sharing that vision with others and working with them to achieve everyone's goals while improving students' education. It means being active so you can share your knowledge of library resources and skills in teaching IL. It means promoting library resources, technology, and services to raise your visibility. It means supporting the curriculum goals of your school in every way you can. Leadership encompasses all you do.

Finally, you are the most important piece in the value puzzle. Your skill, knowledge, professionalism, dedication, commitment, care, and concern touch all aspects of your library's value. What you do provides the strong foundation from which you build your library, embrace change, collaborate with teachers, and lead the library program to improve your students' lives. What you do is invaluable.

Vocabulary

annual reports	Likert scale
collaboration	output measure
data analysis	quantitative assessment
formative assessments	return on investment
input measures	summative assessments
KWL	surveys
leadership	

Questions

Is there an upper limit on the cost per reference question ratio, and if so, would you eliminate reference services? If not, what actions would you take to lower the cost per reference question ratio?

If you were conducting a peer evaluation of a colleague's reference work, what two aspects of their performance would you consider the most important and why? How would you let them know if they were doing a poor job?

In a one-minute formative assessment of an IL instruction session, what questions would you ask, when would you ask them, and why?

Assignment

Use Google Forms to create a customer satisfaction survey for your library. It should cover three aspects (services, collections, resources, etc.) of your library that you consider the most important to have feedback from customers. Justify the aspects you choose to include and the ones you excluded. Have 10 classmates take the survey, and then write a report about the results received.

Bibliography

"2013 BrandZ Top 100." 2014. *MillwardBrown*. Accessed February 27, 2014. http://www.millwardbrown.com/brandz/Top_100_Global_Brands.aspx.

"AASL Learning4Life Lesson Plan Database." 2013. Accessed August 8, 2013. http://aasl.jesandco.org/.

"About Ipl2." 2012. *Ipl2*. http://www.ipl.org/div/about/.

Alexa. 2013a. "Alexa Top 500 Global Sites." *Alexa*. Accessed July 2, 2013. http://www.alexa.com/topsites/global.

Alexa. 2013b. "Pinterest.com Site Info." *Alexa*. Accessed August 12, 2013. http://www.alexa.com/siteinfo/pinterest.com.

Alexander, Carter. 1939. "Co-Operation in Teaching Elementary-School Pupils to Use Library Materials." *The Elementary School Journal* 39 (6): 452–459. doi:10.2307/997705.

American Association of School Librarians. 2007. "Standards for the 21st-Century Learner." *American Association of School Librarians*. Accessed June 22, 2013. http://www.ala.org/ala/mgrps/divs/aasl/guidelinesandstandards/learningstandards/AASL_LearningStandards.pdf.

American Association of School Librarians. 2013. "AASL Learning Standards & Common Core State Standards Crosswalk." *American Association of School Librarians*. Accessed June 23, 2013. http://www.ala.org/aasl/standards-guidelines/crosswalk.

Anderson, Nate. 2008. "Using Crowdsourced Librarians to Outsmart Google." *Ars Technica*. Accessed November 11, 2013. http://arstechnica.com/uncategorized/2008/11/using-crowdsourced-librarians-to-out-google-google/.

Asher, Andrew D., Lynda M. Duke, and Suzanne Wilson. 2013. "Paths of Discovery: Comparing the Search Effectiveness of EBSCO Discovery Service, Summon, Google Scholar, and Conventional Library Resources." *College & Research Libraries* 74 (5) (September 1): 464–488.

"Best Global Brands 2012." 2013. *Interbrand*. Accessed September 26, 2013. http://www.interbrand.com/en/best-global-brands/2012/Best-Global-Brands-2012-Brand-View.aspx.

"Big6 Skills Overview." 2013. *The Big6*. Accessed June 21, 2013. http://big6.com/pages/about/big6-skills-overview.php.

"Bit." 2013. *The Oxford Companion to the Mind Oxford Reference*. Accessed June 9, 2013. http://www.oxfordreference.com.proxy.li.suu.edu:2048/view/10.1093/acref/9780198662242.001.0001/acref-9780198662242-e-114#.

Blakeman, Karen. 2010. "All Change on the Search Front." *Online* 34 (2): 44–47.

Bogart, Dave, ed. 2012. *Library and Book Trade Almanac*. Medford, NJ: Information Today, Inc.

Breeding, Marshall. 2011. "Automation Companies in United States and Canada." *Library Technology Guides*. Accessed September 25, 2013. http://www.librarytechnology.org/companies.pl.

Britannica Editors. 2012. "Change: It's Okay. Really." *Britannica Blog*. Accessed March 13, 2013. http://www.britannica.com/blogs/2012/03/change/.

Brunner, Borgna. 2008. "Everest Almanac: Adjusting to Everest's New Height." *Infoplease*. Access February 27, 2017. http://www.infoplease.com/spot/everest-height1.html.

Burkholder, Joel. 2010. "Redefining Sources as Social Acts: Genre Theory in Information Literacy Instruction." *Library Philosophy and Practice (e-Journal)*. Accessed September 30, 2013. http://digitalcommons.unl.edu/libphilprac/413.

Casson, Lionel. 2001. *Libraries in the Ancient World*. New Haven: Yale University Press.

Chan, Lois Mai. 1994. *Cataloging and Classification: An Introduction*. 2nd ed. New York: McGraw-Hill.

Chandler, Daniel, and Rod Munday. 2011. "Information:" *A Dictionary of Media and Communication Oxford Reference*. Oxford: Oxford University Press. Accessed June 8, 2013. http://www.oxfordreference.com.proxy.li.suu.edu:2048/view/10.1093/acref/9780199568758.001.0001/acref-9780199568758-e-1320?skey=2jZMt6&result=1&q=.

Christensen, Joanne, Fawn Morgan, and Janae Kinikin. 2013. "An Online Information Skills Tutorial." *School Library Monthly* 29 (5): 8–10.

Coates, Heather. 2013. "Exploring the Disconnect Between Information Literacy Skills and Self-Estimates of Ability in First-Year Community College Students." *Evidence Based Library and Information Practice* 8 (2): 264–266.

"Comparison of Screencasting Software." 2013. *Wikipedia, the Free Encyclopedia*. Accessed August 9, 2013. http://en.wikipedia.org/w/index.php?itle=Comparison_of_screencasting_software&oldid=566288885.

"A Computing Pioneer Looks to the Next Frontier." 2013. *Discover* (August): 25.

Conference, American Library Association, American Library Association General Meeting, and American Library Association. 1907. *Papers and Proceedings of the Twenty-ninth Annual Meeting of the American Library Association*, 334. Asheville, NC: American Library Association. Accessed October 28, 2013. http://books.google.com/books?id=kA8bAAAAMAAJ.

Cooke, Rachel, and Danielle Rosenthal. 2011. "Students Use More Books after Library Instruction: An Analysis of Undergraduate Paper Citations." *College & Research Libraries* 72 (4) (July 1): 332–343.

Cox, Monica F., and Angie Androit. 2009. "Mentor and Undergraduate Student Comparisons of Students' Research Skills." *Journal of STEM Education* 10 (1 & 2) (June). Accessed April 23, 2013. http://www.academia.edu/445581/Mentor_and_Undergraduate_Student_Comparisons_of_Students_Research_Skills.

Creative Commons. 2013. "About the Licenses." *Creative Commons*. Accessed July 30, 2013. http://creativecommons.org/licenses/.

"Critical Thinking." 1996. *Philosophy of Education: An Encyclopedia*. London: Routledge. Accessed October 28, 2013. Credo Reference.

Crockett, Lee, Ian Jukes, and Andrew Churches. 2011. *Literacy Is Not Enough: 21st-Century Fluencies for the Digital Age*. [Kelowna, BC]; [Thousand Oaks, CA]: 21st Century Fluency Project; Corwin.

Dalrymple, Connie. 2002. "Perceptions and Practices of Learning Styles in Library Instruction." *College & Research Libraries* 63 (3): 261–273.

Daw, David. 2012. "How to Get Started Screencasting." *TechHive*. Accessed July 24, 2013. http://www.techhive.com/article/259598/how_to_get _started_screencasting.html.

Dempsey, Judy. 2011. "German Defense Minister Karl-Theodor Zu Guttenberg Resigns." *The New York Times*, March 1, sec. World / Europe. Accessed May 2, 2011. http://www.nytimes.com/2011/03/02/world/Europe/ 02germany.html?cp=1&sq=Karl-Theodor%20zu%20Guttenberg&st=cse.

Dow, Mirah J., Jacqueline McMahon Lakin, and Stephen C. Court. 2012. "School Librarian Staffing Levels and Student Achievement as Represented in 2006– 2009 Kansas Annual Yearly Progress Data." *School Library Research (SLR)* 15. Accessed November 5, 2012. http://www.ala.org/aasl/slr.

"The Earliest Surviving Detailed Bibliographical Entries." 2013. *Jeremy Norman's from Cave Paintings to the Internet*. Accessed July 23, 2013. http://www .historyofinformation.com/expanded.php?id=3212.

Eisenberg, Michael. 2012. "Summon the Future with Dr. Mike Eisenberg." Webinar. Recorded Sessions—*SerialSolutions*. Accessed September 19, 2013. http:// www.serialssolutions.com/en/webinars/recorded/.

Ennis, R. H. 2012. "Definition of Critical Thinking." *Criticalthinking.NET*. Accessed June 24, 2013. http://www.criticalthinking.net/definition.html.

Eryaman, Mustafa Yunus, and Salih Zeki Genc. 2013. "Learning Theories." In *Encyclopedia of Curriculum Studies*, edited by Craig Kridel. Thousand Oaks, CA: SAGE Publications, Inc. Accessed May 14, 2013. http://knowledge .sagepub.com/view/curriculumstudies/n289.xml.

Ferrer-Vinent, Ignacio J., and Christy A. Carello. 2011. "The Lasting Value of an Embedded, First-Year, Biology Library Instruction Program." *Science & Technology Libraries* 30 (3) (July): 254–266. doi:10.1080/0194262X .2011.592789.

Georgas, Helen. 2013. "Google vs. the Library: Student Preferences and Perceptions When Doing Research Using Google and a Federated Search Tool." *Portal: Libraries and the Academy* 13 (2): 165–185.

Gillispie, Charles. 1970a. "Boole, George:" *Dictionary of Scientific Biography*. New York: Scribner.

Gillispie, Charles. 1970b. "Venn, John:" *Dictionary of Scientific Biography*. New York: Scribner.

Giustini, Dean. 2008. "Utilizing Learning Theories in the Digital Age: An Introduction for Health Librarians." *Journal of the Canadian Health Libraries Association* 29 (3): 109–115. doi:10.5596/c08-028.

Glazer, Sarah. 2013. "Plagiarism and Cheating." *CQ Researcher by CQ Press* 23 (1) (January 4). Accessed July 8, 2013. http://library.cqpress.com/cqresearcher/ cqresrre2013010400.

Godbold, Natalya. 2013. "Beyond Information Seeking: A General Model of Information Behaviour." *Information* Research 11 (4). Accessed May 10, 2013. http://informationr.net/ir/11-4/paper269.html.

Grassian, Esther S., and Joan R. Kaplowitz. 2001. *Information Literacy Instruction: Theory and Practice*. New York: Neal-Schuman.

Harper, Meghan. 2011. *Reference Sources and Services for Youth.* New York: Neal-Schuman Publishers.

Head, Alison J., and Michael B. Eisenberg. 2009a. "Finding Context: What Today's College Students Say About Conducting Research in the Digital Age." The Information School, University of Washington, Seattle, WA. Accessed September 10, 2012. http://projectinfolit.org/pdfs/PIL_ProgressReport_2_2009.pdf.

Head, Alison J., and Michael B. Eisenberg. 2009b. "Lessons Learned: How College Students Seek Information in the Digital Age." The Information School, University of Washington, Seattle, WA. Accessed September 10, 2012. http://projectinfolit.org/pdfs/PIL_Fall2009_finalv_YR1_12_2009v2.pdf.

Head, Alison J., and Michael B. Eisenberg. 2010a. "Assigning Inquiry: How Handouts for Research Assignments Guide Today's College Students." The Information School, University of Washington, Seattle, WA. Accessed September 10, 2012. http://projectinfolit.org/pdfs/PIL_Handout_Study_finalvJuly_2010.pdf.

Head, Alison J., and Michael B. Eisenberg. 2010b. "Truth Be Told: How College Students Evaluate and Use Information in the Digital Age." The Information School, University of Washington, Seattle, WA. Accessed September 10, 2012. http://projectinfolit.org/pdfs/PIL_Fall2010_Survey_FullReport1.pdf.

Heinström, Jannica. 2006. "Fast Surfing for Availability or Deep Diving into Quality—Motivation and Information Seeking among Middle and High School Students." *Information Research* 11 (4) (July). Accessed October 28, 2013. http://InformationR.net/ir/11-4/paper265.html.

Hernon, Peter, and Charles R. McClure. 1986. "Unobtrusive Reference Testing: The 55 Percent Rule. (cover Story)." *Library Journal* 111 (7) (April 15): 37.

Hirtle, Peter B. 2013. "Copyright Term and the Public Domain in the United States." *Cornell Copyright Information Center.* Accessed July 30, 2013. http://copyright.cornell.edu/resources/publicdomain.cfm.

Hollins, E. 2012. "Learning Styles:" *Encyclopedia of Diversity in Education.* Thousand Oaks, CA: SAGE Publications. Accessed April 23, 2013. http://knowledge.sagepub.com/view/diversityineducation/n434.xml?rskey=nQ03ei&row=1.

"How Opal Mehta Got Kissed, Got Wild, and Got a Life." 2013. *Wikipedia, the Free Encyclopedia.* Accessed July 31, 2013. http://en.wikipedia.org/w/index.php?itle=How_Opal_Mehta_Got_Kissed,_Got_Wild,_and_Got_a_Life&oldid=566171893.

"How Search Works: The Story." 2013. *Inside Search.* Accessed September 25, 2013. http://www.google.com/intl/en/insidesearch/howsearchworks/thestory/index.html.

"Humanism." 2013. *Learning Theories.* Accessed August 6, 2013. http://www.learning-theories.com/humanism.html.

"Humanistic Education." 2013. *Wikipedia, the Free Encyclopedia.* Accessed August 6, 2013. http://en.wikipedia.org/w/index.php?itle=Humanistic_education&oldid=566525344.

IFLA. 2013. "IFLA Digital Reference Guidelines." Accessed July 1, 2013. http://www.ifla.org/publications/ifla-digital-reference-guidelines.

"In the States." 2012. *Common Core State Standards Initiative.* Accessed June 22, 2013. http://www.corestandards.org/in-the-states.

"Integrated Library System." 2013. *Wikipedia, the Free Encyclopedia.* Accessed September 20, 2013. http://en.wikipedia.org/w/index.php?itle=Integrated_library_system&oldid=569234019.

iParadigms. 2013. "Turnitin—Overview." *Turnitin.* Accessed July 31, 2013. http://turnitin.com/en_us/features/overview.

Ipri, Tom. 2010. "Introducing Transliteracy." *College & Research Libraries News* 71 (10) (November): 532–567.

Julien, Heidi. 2005. "Education for Information Literacy Instruction: A Global Perspective." *Journal of Education for Library & Information Science* 46 (3): 210–216.

Jump, Paul, and Annabel Symington. 2013. "The Best Policy?" *Times Education Supplement,* May 16, sec. Feature.

Kachel, Debra E. 2013. "School Library Research Summarized: A Graduate Class Project." School Library & Information Technologies Department, Mansfield University, Mansfield, PA. Accessed September 10, 2013. http://sl-it .mansfield.edu/upload/MU-LibAdvoBklt2013.pdf.

Kaplowitz, Joan. 2008. "The Psychology of Learning: Connecting Theory to Practice." In *Information Literacy Instruction Handbook,* edited by Christopher N. Cox and Elizabeth Blakesley, 26–49. Chicago: Association of College and Research Libraries.

Kaske, Neal, and Julie Arnold. 2002. "An Unobtrusive Evaluation of Online Real Time Library Reference Services." Paper presented at the Library Research Round Table, American Library Association Annual Conference, Atlanta, Georgia. Accessed September 27, 2012. http://www.lib.umd.edu/groups/ digref/kaskearnoldunobtrusive.html.

"Keyword (linguistics)." 2013. *Wikipedia, the Free Encyclopedia.* Accessed September 17, 2013. http://en.wikipedia.org/w/index.php?itle=Keyword _(linguistics)&oldid=541704022.

"Keyword, N." 2013. *OED Online.* Oxford University Press. Accessed September 17, 2013. http://www.oed.com/view/Entry/312961.

Lance, Keith Curry. 2002. "Impact of School Library Media Programs on Academic Achievement." *Teacher Librarian* 29 (3) (February): 29–34.

Lance, Keith Curry, and Linda Hofschire. 2012. "Change in School Librarian Staffing Linked with Change in CSAP Reading Performance, 2005 to 2011." *Library Research Service.* Accessed March 8, 2012. http://www.lrs.org/ news/2012/01/17/change-in-school-librarian-staffing-linked-with-change -in-csap-reading-performance-2005-to-2011/.

Langhorne, Mary Jo, Denise Rehmke, and Iowa City Community School District. 2011. *Developing 21st Century Literacies: A K-12 School Library Curriculum Blueprint with Sample Lessons.* New York: Neal-Schuman Publishers.

"Learning Styles." 2013. *Wikipedia, the Free Encyclopedia.* Accessed April 23, 2013. http://en.wikipedia.org/w/index.php?itle=Learning_styles&oldid =551426651.

Library Research Service. 2013a. "Library User Survey Templates & How-Tos." *Library Research Service.* Accessed October 29, 2013. http://www.lrs.org/ library-user-surveys-on-the-web/.

Library Research Service. 2013b. "School Libraries Impact Studies." *Library Research Service.* Accessed November 8, 2013. http://www.lrs.org/data -tools/school-libraries/impact-studies/.

"List of Search Engines." 2013. *Wikipedia, the Free Encyclopedia.* Accessed September 26, 2013. http://en.wikipedia.org/w/index.php?itle=List_of _search_engines&oldid=571236991.

List-Handley, Carla. 2008. "Teaching as Performance." In *Information Literacy Instruction Handbook,* edited by Christopher N. Cox and Elizabeth Blakesley, 65-73. Chicago: Association of College and Research Libraries.

"Literate, Adj. and N." 2013. *OED Online.* Oxford University Press. Accessed April 16, 2013. http://www.oed.com/view/Entry/109070?redirectedFrom =literate#eid.

Lloyd, Annemaree. 2010. "Framing Information Literacy as Information Practice: Site Ontology and Practice Theory." *Journal of Documentation* 66 (2) (March): 245–258.

Lorenzen, Michael. 2001. "A Brief History of Library Information in the United States of America." *Illinois Libraries* 83 (2): 8–18.

Lown, Cory, Tito Sierra, and Josh Boyer. 2013. "How Users Search the Library from a Single Search Box." *College & Research Libraries* 74 (3) (May 1): 227–241.

MacDonald, Cynthia, and Rob Darrow. 2013. "Information Literacy Models and Comparison Chart." Accessed April 23, 2013. http://infopeople.org/sites/all/files/past/2004/k12infolit/handout_infolitmodels.pdf.

MacLeod, Colin M. 2004. "Individual Differences in Learning and Memory." In *Learning and Memory,* edited by John H. Byrne, 2nd ed., 251–253. New York: Macmillan Reference USA.

"Main Page." 2013. *Wikipedia, the Free Encyclopedia.* Accessed July 24, 2013. http://en.wikipedia.org/w/index.php?itle=Main_Page&oldid=560327612.

Martin, Jason. 2008. "The Information Seeking Behavior of Undergraduate Education Majors: Does Library Instruction Play a Role?" *Evidence Based Library and Information Practice* 3 (4) (December 13): 4–17.

Matthews, Joseph R. 2011. "What's the Return on ROI? The Benefits and Challenges of Calculating Your Library's Return on Investment." *Library Leadership & Management* 25 (1) (January): 1–14.

McCrink, Carmen L., and Teri D. Melton. 2009. "Critical Thinking." In *Encyclopedia of the Social and Cultural Foundations of Education Encyclopedia of the Social and Cultural Foundations of Education.* Thousand Oaks, CA: SAGE Publications, Inc. Accessed April 23, 2013. http://knowledge.sagepub.com/view/foundations/n98.xml.

McGraw-Hill Dictionary of Scientific and Technical Terms. 2013. "Information:" *McGraw-Hill Dictionary of Scientific and Technical Terms.* Accessed June 10, 2013.

Meola, Marc. 2004. "Chucking the Checklist: A Contextual Approach to Teaching Undergraduates Web-Site Evaluation." *Portal: Libraries and the Academy* 4 (3): 331–344.

Merriam-Webster, Inc. 2010a. "Merriam-Webster's Collegiate Dictionary, Eleventh Edition." *Merriam-Webster Online.* Accessed July, 24, 2013. http://www.merriam-webster.com/cgi-bin/book.pl?c11.htm.

Merriam-Webster, Inc. 2010b. "Webster's Third New International Dictionary, Unabridged." *Merriam-Webster Online.* Accessed July 24, 2013. http://www.merriam-webster.com/cgi-bin/book.pl?w3.htm.

Merriam-Webster, Inc. 2013. "Literate:" *Merriam-Webster Dictionary.* Accessed April 16, 2013. http://www.merriam-webster.com/dictionary/literate.

Merriam-Webster, Inc. 2013a. "Information:" *Merriam-Webster Dictionary.* Accessed June 10, 2013. http://www.merriam-webster.com/dictionary/information.

Merriam-Webster, Inc. 2013b. "Plagiarize:" *Merriam-Webster Online Dictionary.* Accessed July 31, 2013. http://www.merriam-webster.com/dictionary/plagiarized?how=0&t=1375297892.

Merriam-Webster, Inc. 2013c. "Key Word:" *Merriam-Webster Dictionary.* Accessed September 17, 2013. http://www.merriam-webster.com/dictionary/keyword.

Merriam-Webster, Inc. 2013d. "Catalog:" *Merriam-Webster Dictionary.* Accessed September 20, 2013. http://www.merriam-webster.com/dictionary/catalog.

Merriam-Webster, Inc. 2013e. "Facet:" *Merriam-Webster Dictionary.* Accessed September 26, 2013. http://www.merriam-webster.com/dictionary/facet.

Mery, Yvonne, Jill Newby, and Ke Peng. 2012. "Why One-Shot Information Literacy Sessions Are Not the Future of Instruction: A Case for Online Credit Courses." *College & Research Libraries* 73 (4) (July 1): 366–377.

Minkel, Walter. 2002. "Web of Deceit." *School Library Journal* 48 (4) (April): 50–54.

Monroe, Wanda. 2005. "Libraries Return on Investment Study." *Library Mosaics* 16 (6) (December 11): 12–13.

Morris, Rebecca J. 2012. "Find Where You Fit in the Common Core, or the Time I Forgot about Librarians and Reading." *Teacher Librarian* 39 (5) (June): 8–12.

Niemeler, Kathy. 1983. "Telecom Primer." *Information Today*, November, 16–17.

Olof Sundin, Helena Francke. 2009. "In Search of Credibility: Pupils' Information Practices in Learning Environments." *Information Research* 14 (4) (December). Accessed June 26, 2013. http://informationr.net.proxy.li.suu.edu:2048/ir/14-4/paper418.html.

"Online Tutorials." 2010. *Library Success: A Best Practices Wiki.* Accessed May 4, 2013. http://www.libsuccess.org/index.php?itle=Online_Tutorials#Windows.

Oxford English Dictionary. 2013. *Oxford English Dictionary.* Oxford University Press. Accessed http://www.oed.com/.

Pariser, Eli. 2011. "Beware Online 'Filter Bubbles'." *TED Talks.* Accessed October 11, 2013. http://www.ted.com/talks/eli_pariser_beware_online _filter_bubbles.html.

"Pathways to Knowledge." 2013. *Virtual Information Inquiry.* Accessed June 21, 2013. http://virtualinquiry.com/inquiry/pathways.htm.

Phan, Tai, Laura Hardesty, Jamie Hug, and Cindy Scheckells. 2011. "Academic Libraries: 2010. First Look." *National Center for Education Statistics.* Accessed July 22, 2013. http://nces.ed.gov/pubs2012/2012365.pdf#page=21.

"Presidential Committee on Information Literacy: Final Report." 2013. Accessed April 23, 2013. http://www.ala.org/acrl/publications/whitepapers/presidential.

"REACTS Stripling and Pitts Research Process Model." 2011. *Virtual Information Inquiry.* Accessed June 21, 2013. http://virtualinquiry.com/inquiry/ stripling.htm.

Reference and User Services Association. 2004. "Guidelines for Behavioral Performance of Reference and Information Service Providers." Accessed June 28, 2013. http://www.ala.org/rusa/resources/guidelines/guidelines behavioral.

"Reliability of Wikipedia." 2013. *Wikipedia, the Free Encyclopedia.* Accessed July 24, 2013. http://en.wikipedia.org/w/index.php?itle=Reliability_of _Wikipedia&oldid=565648834.

Rethlefsen, Melissa L. 2008. "Easy ? Right." *Library Journal* 133 (July 2): 12–14.

Richardson, J. V., Jr. 2002. "Reference Is Better Than We Thought." *Library Journal* 127 (7) (April 15): 41–42.

Salony, Mary F. 1995. "The History of Bibliographic Instruction: Changing Trends from Books to the Electronic World." *Reference Librarian* 24 (51/52) (November 3): 31–51.

Sattler, Sebastian, Peter Graeff, and Sebastian Willen. 2013. "Explaining the Decision to Plagiarize: An Empirical Test of the Interplay Between Rationality, Norms, and Opportunity." *Deviant Behavior* 34 (6) (June): 444–463.

Schneider, Karen G. 2000. "The Distributed Librarian: Live, Online, Real-Time Reference." *American Libraries* 31 (10) (November): 64–66.

"School Libraries." 2013. *ERIC Thesaurus.* Accessed September 18, 2013. http:// eric.ed.gov/?t=school+libraries&ts=on&td=on&ti=School+Libraries.

SCONUL Working Group on Information Literacy. 2011. "The SCONUL Seven Pillars of Information Literacy: Core Model for Higher Education." Accessed February 27, 2014. http://www.sconul.ac.uk/sites/default/files/documents/ coremodel.pdf.

"Search Engine Update." 2012. *Online* 36 (1) (February 1): 13–13.

Shannon, Donna M. 2012. "Perceptions of School Library Programs and School Librarians." *Teacher Librarian* 39 (3) (February): 17–22.

Shera, Jesse Hauk. 1976. *Introduction to Library Science: Basic Elements of Library Service.* Littleton, Colo.: Libraries Unlimited.

Siegler, M. G. 2013. "Eric Schmidt: Every 2 Days We Create as Much Information as We Did Up to 2003 | *TechCrunch.*" TechCrunch. Accessed June 17, 2013. http://techcrunch.com/2010/08/04/schmidt-data/.

Small, Ruth V. 2012. *Teaching for Inquiry: Engaging the Learner Within.* New York: Neal-Schuman Publishers.

Springshare. 2013. "Best of Home." *Guide Community.* Accessed August 12, 2013. http://bestof.libguides.com/home.

"The Standards." 2012. *Common Core State Standards Initiative.* Accessed June 22, 2013. http://www.corestandards.org/the-standards.

"Student Achievement." 2013. *AASL Essential Links.* Accessed October 8, 2013. http://www.aasl.ala.org/essentiallinks/index.php?itle=Student_Achievement.

Sullivan, Danny. 1998. "Ask Jeeves: Asking Questions to Give You Answers." *Search Engine Watch.* Accessed October 2, 2013. http://searchenginewatch.com/article/2067467/Ask-Jeeves-Asking-Questions-To-Give-You-Answers.

"Teacher Resources." 2013. *Library of Congress.* Accessed August 8, 2013. http://www.loc.gov/teachers/.

Teague-Rector, Susan, and Jimmy Ghaphery. 2008. "Designing Search: Effective Search Interfaces for Academic Library Web Sites."*Journal of Web Librarianship* 2 (4): 479–492.

Tenopir, Carol. 2004. "Rethinking Virtual Reference." *Library Journal* 129 (18) (November 11): 34.

Thomson Reuters. 2013. Endnote. *Thomson Reuters.* Accessed July 31, 2013. http://endnote.com/.

Todd, Ross J. 2006. "From Information to Knowledge: Charting and Measuring Changes in Students' Knowledge of a Curriculum Topic." *Information Research* 11 (4) (July). Accessed May 10, 2013. http://informationr.net/ir/11-4/paper264.html.

Todd, Ross J., Carol A. Gordon, and Ya-Ling Lu. 2011. "One Common Goal: Student Learning." Report of Findings and Recommendations of the New Jersey School Library Survey: Phase 2, Center for International Scholarship in School Libraries, Rutgers, New Brunswick, NJ. Accessed November 6, 2013. http://www.njasl.info/cissl-study/.

U.S. Copyright Office. 2008. "Copyright Basics." United States Copyright Office. Accessed April 26, 2011. http://www.copyright.gov/circs/circ1.pdf.

U.S. Copyright Office. 2009. "Fair Use." U.S. *Copyright Office—Fair Use.* Accessed April 26, 2011. http://www.copyright.gov/fls/fl102.html.

Vucovich, Lee A., Valerie S. Gordon, Nicole Mitchell, and Lisa A. Ennis. 2013. "Is the Time and Effort worth It? One Library's Evaluation of Using Social Networking Tools for Outreach." *Medical Reference Services Quarterly* 32 (1) (January): 12–25.

Webber, Sheila, and Bill Johnston. 2006. "Information Literacy: Definitions and Models." Accessed September 27, 2012. http://dis.shef.ac.uk/literacy/definitions.htm.

Weiner, John M. 2011. "Is There a Difference Between Critical Thinking and Information Literacy?" *Journal of Information Literacy* 5 (2) (November 30): 81–92.

"Wikipedia:size Comparisons." 2013. *Wikipedia, the Free Encyclopedia.* Accessed July 24, 2013. http://en.wikipedia.org/w/index.php?itle=Wikipedia:Size_comparisons&oldid=562880212.

Wilson, T. D. 2006. "A Re-examination of Information Seeking Behaviour in the Context of Activity Theory." *Information Research* 11 (4) (July). Accessed May 10, 2013. http://informationr.net/ir/11-4/paper260.html.

Wladawsky-Berger, Irving. 2012. "Why CIOs Desperately Need a Technology-Literate Society." *WSJ Blogs—The CIO Report.* Accessed September 24, 2012. http://blogs.wsj.com/cio/2012/09/23/why-cios-desperately-need-a-technology-literate-society/.

Wolchover, Natalie. 2013. "How Accurate Is Wikipedia?" *Livescience.com.* Accessed July 24, 2013. http://www.livescience.com/32950-how-accurate-is-wikipedia.html.

Wong, Shun Han Rebekah, and Dianne Cmor. 2011. "Measuring Association Between Library Instruction and Graduation GPA." *College & Research Libraries* 72 (5) (September): 464–473.

"The World Almanac and Book of Facts." 2013. *The World Almanac.* Accessed July 23, 2013. http://www.worldalmanac.com/world-almanac.aspx.

World Intellectual Property Organization. 2011. "What Is Intellectual Property?" 2011. *World Intellectual Property Organization.* Accessed June 28, 2013. http://www.wipo.int/about-ip/en/.

Zickuhr, Kathryn, Lee Rainie, and Kristen Purcell. 2013. "Younger Americans' Library Habits and Expectations." *Pew Internet Libraries.* Accessed July 10, 2013. http://libraries.pewinternet.org/2013/06/25/younger-Americans-library-services/.

Zink, Steven D. 1977. "Computer Output Microform Library Catalog: a Survey." Arlington, VA: Educational Resources Information Center, 15p. Accessed September 20, 2013. http://search.proquest.com.ezproxy.lib.utah.edu/lisa/docview/57157421/140A2E16A4920A01AEA/1?accountid=14677.

Index

About the Author

SCOTT LANNING is professor of library media and reference librarian at Southern Utah University, Cedar City, UT. His published works include Libraries Unlimited's *Essential Reference Services for Today's School Media Specialists* and *Concise Guide to Information Literacy*. Lanning holds a master's degree in library science from Northern Illinois University.